SCIENCE, TECHNOLOGY
AND FREE TRADE

SCIENCE, TECHNOLOGY AND FREE TRADE

Edited by

John de la Mothe and Louis Marc Ducharme

Pinter Publishers
London & New York

© The editors and contributors 1990

First published in Great Britain in 1990 by
Pinter Publishers Limited
25 Floral Street, London WC2E 9DS

British Library Cataloguing in Publication Data

A CIP catalogue record for this book is available from the
British Library

ISBN 0 86187 728 4

Library of Congress Cataloging-in-Publication Data

Science, technology, and free trade / edited by John de la Mothe and
  Louis Marc Ducharme.
      p.   cm.
   Includes bibliographical references and index.
   ISBN 0–86187–728–4
   1. Free trade.   2. Science and state.   3. Technology and state.
I. De La Mothe, John.   II. Ducharme, Louis Marc.
HF1713.S44   1990
382′.71——dc20   90–37104
                                                         CIP

Photoset in North Wales by
Derek Doyle & Associates, Mold, Clwyd.
Printed and bound in Great Britain by
Biddles Ltd, Guildford and Kings Lynn,

To
Donna and Michèle

Contents

Section 5: Conclusions

Notes on contributors

The Editors

John de la Mothe is a social scientist who was educated at Concordia, Oxford and Sussex Universities (the Science Policy Research Unit). He teaches science policy and R&D management in the Graduate Faculty of Administration at the University of Ottawa. *Louis Marc Ducharme* is an economist who was educated at l'Université de Montréal and Sussex University (the Science Policy Research Unit). He lectures regularly on technological diffusion and the use of science indicators. Both can be reached at the Faculty of Administration, University of Ottawa, P.O. Box 142, 275 Nicholas Street, Ottawa, Canada.

The Authors

Laura D'Andrea Tyson is Visiting Fellow at Harvard University's School of Business.

Mark Dodgson is Research Fellow at the Science Policy Research Unit, University of Sussex.

Giovanni Dosi is Professor of Applied Economics at the University of Rome, 'La Sapienza' and visiting fellow at the Science Policy Research Unit, University of Sussex.

Chris Freeman is Professor Emeritus at the Science Policy Research Unit, University of Sussex, and Visiting Fellow at the Maastricht Economic Research Institute on Innovation and Technology, University of Limburg.

Luke Georghiou is Director of the Programme for Research on the Evaluation of Science and Technology, University of Manchester.

Michael Gibbons is Director of the Technology Transfer and Research Office at the University of Manchester and Professor in the Programme for Research on the Evaluation of Science and Technology.

Christopher Hill is Director of the Manufacturing Forum, National Academy of Science, Washington.

Stan Metcalfe is Professor of Economics, University of Manchester.

Pari Patel is Research Fellow at the Science Policy Research Unit, University of Sussex.

Keith Pavitt is Deputy Director of the Science Policy Research Unit, University of Sussex.

Roy Rothwell is Senior Fellow and Director of the Management of Technology Programme at the Science Policy Research Unit, University of Sussex.

Luc Soete is Professor of International Economics at the University of Limburg, the Netherlands and Director of the Maastricht Economic Research Institute on Innovation and Technology, University of Limburg.

David Teece is Professor of Business Administration at the University of California at Berkeley.

John Zysman is Professor of Political Science and Director of the Berkeley Roundtable on the International Economy at the University of California at Berkeley.

Preface

Christopher Freeman

The theory of international trade has traditionally played an extremely important role in the development of economic theory generally. It has also had a major influence on the policies of governments and on international relations. In fact there has seldom been an area of economic policy where pure theory was so frequently invoked either to justify or to condemn specific policies of one country or another.

Adam Smith's onslaught on mercantilism and Ricardo's theory of comparative advantage became a part of the core doctrine of classical economics. They provided the foundation for the Manchester School's crusading campaign for international free trade in the nineteenth century. To this day free trade in Manchester stands as an enduring monument to this ideology and to its dominance in the leading industrial city in the great days of Britain's Industrial Revolution. Free trade was much more than a sophisticated economic theory; it was also a political ideology with religious overtones.

Although there has been some mathematical refinement of the classical models through the Heckscher–Ohlin theorem and other more recent neo-classical work, the ideology of the Manchester School remains to this day the essential theoretical underpinning for the very existence of the General Agreement on Tariff and Trade (GATT) and for its extensive regulatory activities. Yet despite its enormous and continuing influence there has seldom been a theory either in the natural or the social sciences which has had so little empirical verification.

At a time when the post-war GATT arrangements are subject to increasing strains and new regional trading arrangements are developing, this book is therefore a timely reminder of the interdependence of theory and policy-making, and of the need for theory to provide a reliable guide to new developments in the world economy. Never was it more necessary to re-examine fundamentals and this book provides just such a searching re-examination.

In this of course it follows in a long tradition. Despite its pre-eminence the free trade doctrine has always been challenged by a variety of 'heretics', from Friedrich List to Posner, Vernon and other contemporary advocates of 'technology gap' theories. There is food for thought in the fact that the most zealous advocates of free trade orthodoxy have tended to be in the countries which had achieved world economic dominance whereas the critics were often located in 'catching up' or 'developing' countries.

The Manchester School flourished when British exports dominated world trade in textiles, steam engines, railway equipment, machine tools and many other manufactured goods. After a period of competitive protectionism in the depression

years of the 1930s, the USA turned its back on protectionism in the post-war years
and used its enormous influence to inspire an international regulatory regime which
enshrined free trade once again as the dominant doctrine. This was the period in
the 1940s and 1950s when the USA still dominated world export markets,
especially in the mass production industries of automobiles and consumer
durables, in petro-chemicals, process plant and machinery. Now that US
dominance has been undermined by Japanese and German competition, and both
Britain and USA have developed intractable deficits in their trade in manufactures,
there is increasing pressure to amend the rules, to make exceptions and to question
some aspects of the theory. Just as in the nineteenth century British industrialists
and economists tended to blame 'unfair' German trade competition for their loss of
market share, today it is Japanese trading practices which come in for sustained
attack. However, increasingly it is the Germans and Japanese who now endorse the
ideology of free trade, which they did not follow in the period when they were
overtaking the leaders.

Indeed the major challenge to free trade theory came from the German states
when they were 'newly industrializing countries' (customs union or common
market) in their efforts to overtake Britain. It was Friedrich List who provided the
most convincing alternative to the classical school and to this day he is the *bête
noire* of zealous free traders. He is so often ridiculed as a nationalistic advocate of
protection and the father of the 'infant industry' argument that it is usually
forgotten that he actually believed in free trade. He maintained that free trade was
feasible, however, only among countries which were roughly on an equal level in
terms of wealth and technology.

Britain appeared in the early nineteenth century much as Japan appears today,
as a country with such enormous strength in world markets for advanced products
that it was very hard for the industries of other countries to survive the competition.
List therefore insisted that Germany had first of all to catch up with Britain in terms
of technology. He recognized moreover that such a catching-up process was not a
matter of a few months or years. Nor was it confined to a few products of processes.
Technology accumulation in List's theory was a complex long-term problem
involving strong public policies, as well as many private competitive initiatives.
Many of his proposals were similar to those described in Chapters 7 and 8 of this
book by Hill, Rothwell and Dodgson.

List could indeed be regarded as a forerunner of the theory of 'Schumpeterian
comparative advantage' combined with Ricardian comparative advantage which is
developed in this book, particularly in Chapters 2 and 3. Scientific and technical
institutions were of course less developed in his day than the complex network of
public and private R & D laboratories and related organizations, so well analysed
in Chapters 4, 5 and 6 by Georghiou, Metcalfe, Patel, Pavitt and Teece.
Nevertheless the basic approach to 'technology accumulation' was essentially
similar as is evident from his comment that:

> The present state of the nations is the result of the accumulation of all discoveries,
> inventions, improvements, perfections and exertions of all generations which have lived
> before us; they form the intellectual capital of the present human race, and every
> separate nation is productive only in the proportion in which it has known how to
> appropriate these attainments of former generations and to increase them by its own
> acquirements.

Since the time of List the importance of uneven development in the world economy and the uneven pace of technology accumulation have repeatedly re-emerged as issues which simply cannot be neglected in any satisfactory trade theory. Nor can trade theory be separated from the issues of growth and development, and this book provides an admirable illustration of this proposition. Trade, technology and growth theory are so intimately related that satisfactory progress depends on their integration within one coherent framework.

The authors of the various chapters are all well qualified to develop a critique of orthodox theory. All of them have worked on the role of technical change in competition between firms and countries and it is in this area that traditional trade theory is at its most vulnerable. Soete, Dosi and Pavitt have already made an outstanding contribution both to the critique of mainstream theory and to the development of a more satisfactory alternative. In this book the editors and their colleagues demonstrate beyond reasonable doubt that it is really no longer possible to neglect what they describe as 'Schumpeterian comparative advantage' in the explanation of international trade flows and the long-term shifts in the trade performance of nations.

Section 1:

Introduction

1 Science, technology and free trade: towards an understanding of the new competitive agenda

John de la Mothe and Louis Marc Ducharme

The current orientation of industrialized nations towards free trade and the globalization of research and technology implies a series of deep structural shifts for national policies, corporate strategies and overall economic performance. However, there is little about 'free trade' which is new. For example, conceptually, free trade is a long-standing feature of traditional economic thinking. Within classical economic theory the non-interventionist stance in trade theory and trade policy can be traced as far back as to Adam Smith (1776). Within this framework, perfect competition between private producers is seen as being most efficient. From this premise it follows that state intervention reduces market efficiencies. The case for free trade is thus firmly grounded.

This case is similarly supported by neo-classical theory in its general case for free markets. Considered in these terms, the basic problem of economics is seen to be one of how to allocate scarce resources such as capital, skilled labour and raw materials. The limitation on available resources at any given time forces choices regarding the mix of activities. What the free market offers is a decentralized way of making choices through price mechanisms. When extended to questions of trade, the neo-classical perspective sees market efficiencies as giving absolute advantage.

However, perhaps the most familiar case for free trade arises from the Ricardian and neo-Ricardian principle of comparative advantage in which trade is seen essentially as being a way for countries to benefit from their differences. Because countries differ in resources, skill sets and so on, each country will have a comparative advantage in producing goods for which its particular endowment mix is best suited. Free trade is thus seen as maximizing the comparative advantages of a country while giving it fullest access to a broad mix of desired commodities produced abroad.

As this book argues throughout, however, these traditional trade theories – and the policies they support – are generally incapable of explaining post-war economic and trading performance. Indeed this inadequacy stems in part from the peripheral role which they assign to the restructuring economic power of science and technology. The 'winds of creative destruction' – to use Joseph Schumpeter's phrase – which are represented by basic research, technological and institutional innovation, and technological diffusion, will only increase in importance as we move into the twenty-first century. Thus, as this book suggests, alternative conceptions of trade theory and trade policy can be defined which feature what we call 'Schumpeterian comparative advantage' or 'Schumpeterian efficiencies' and which, if developed theoretically and adopted, promise to enhance significantly the economic performance of trading nations.

In historical terms, policies promoting free trade are not new. The post-war period was dominated by a practical discourse which was strongly in favour of free trade. The consequences of protectionism and the scarcities left by the war were so great that strident pleas for the reduction of trade barriers were institutionalized in the General Agreement on Tariff and Trade (GATT) and legitimated in such international agencies as the World Bank and the Organization for Economic Co-operation and Development (OECD). Thus it was not incidental that from its inception in 1957, the OECD has been committed to lowering trade barriers and to promoting the expansion of world trade on a multilateral and non-discriminating basis. Nevertheless, it should not be surprising that within the post-war context, it was those countries which enjoyed the greatest comparative advantage or competitive edge which argued most strongly in favour of free trade. At that time, they could afford to risk the reduction of protectionist barriers. However, relative comparative advantages are by no means static or permanent, as the case of nineteenth century Britain or the more recent responses of the USA to Europe and Japan illustrate. During periods in which 'swings' of trading strength take place and in which trading and geo-political barriers are reduced, new alliances and new trading blocks often emerge. But they do not happen overnight. [1]

Within the European Economic Community, for example, the Treaty of Rome (1957) under which it was established provided for the creation of a single integrated market which is free of restrictions on the movement of goods. It went well beyond the abolition of tariffs to require the elimination of quantitative restrictions and other measures which have the same effect. However, the elimination of internal obstacles to the movement of goods, capital and services took a long time and has never been entirely achieved, thus attesting to the sheer scale and complexity of the endeavour. Only with the 'Acte unique' (1987) and the political commitment of all twelve countries does the creation of a truly 'single market' within Europe – with all that this signifies – stand a chance of being realized. However, the stakes that are implied in this restructuring are high. Indeed, the creation of free trade zones is not so much associated with the magical harmonization of the world economy as it is with the creation of what is seen as being the necessary structures, alliances and environment for each new trading block to compete.

Thus for corporations and nations alike, free trade is fundamentally about competition. It is not about more equitable distribution of wealth and incomes. It is not about the selfless harmonization of standards and trade barriers. It is not about utopian notions of the evolution of the world's industrialized nations towards a 'post-protectionist' or 'post-industrial' economy. Free trade is about competing. It is about defending existing comparative advantages while developing new ones. And as the reorganization of the European and North American markets makes clear, free trade is about winners and losers. Thus what this book is about is how science and technology − two of the newest, most interrelated and arguably most critical driving forces in the economy − will affect (and themselves be implicated in) the performance of nations and corporations in an increasingly integrated and liberalized market-place.

In coming to an understanding of the new competitive agenda that will face firms and governments, a number of complex and interrelated features will need to be faced. As this book argues:

a new economic paradigm must be developed which focuses on technological opportunities and the cumulativeness of technical change, trade and technological gaps, and Schumpeterian comparative advantage;

trade policies must be developed in such a way as to incorporate both science and technology to achieve more sustainable Schumpeterian efficiencies;

science and technology policies must be developed which draw on, but which do not overburden, national science systems with short-term national priorities. Steps must be taken to ensure the creative potential of the research communities; and

the tension between public science and private intellectual property rights must be made a principal focus of attention for both corporate and university research administrators. Under free trade, the public mandate of the university system is being revised in a way which potentially commodifies the research results of science, scientific personnel and even the culture of science itself.

In the years to come, free trade will redefine the nature of economic (as well as geopolitical) security. It will heighten corporations' awareness of the need to capture value, markets and technologies through new modes (including 'co-operative competition'). It will heighten the importance of governments' policy responses to global, industrial and research challenges. Science and technology will play a major role throughout this redefinition. Understanding the dynamics of science, technology and free trade is essential if we are to determine who the winners will be and how we are best to compete. This is the subject of this book.

Section 2:

Technology and international competitiveness under free trade

2 Technical change theory and international trade competition

Luc Soete

INTRODUCTION

Historians and contemporary practitioners in both industry and government are well aware of the significant influence that technology and innovative activities are having on international competitiveness. From the most recent OECD or UN documents to the various individual countries' international think-thank recommendations, the importance of technical change as 'chronic disturber of existing patterns of comparative advantage'[1] as well as an essential factor in the achievement of the necessary adjustment to structural change resulting from technical change itself[2] is by now well recognized. In a similar way, the most recent Economic Report of the President[3] recognizes the increased 'international scope of science and technology' during the 1980s and subscribes to the view expressed in the earlier Report on US Competitiveness linking directly the erosion of the international competitiveness of the US during the 1960s and 1970s to deficient investment in innovative activity in the USA as compared with its major industrial competitors.[4]

Economists, too, over the past thirty years have become increasingly aware of the importance of technology and innovation. This they have done partly as a result of empirical studies on the determinants of economic growth and trade performance and partly as the result of new insights into international trade theory following on from the formal introduction of imperfect competition in international trade models. While significant progress has been made in the most recent period, analysis has nevertheless been constrained by two major difficulties: inadequate data measuring 'domestic' and international innovative activities and – despite the introduction of some dynamic features – the continual reliance on a theoretical framework in which *static* distributional issues remained the centre piece of trade analysis.

With regard to the latter, as Vernon noted in his introduction to the influential readings on *The Technology Factor in International Trade*, 'researchers have an extraordinary capacity to screen out the evidence that does not fit well with their preconceptions; to relegate uncomfortable observations to the dustbins of the unconscious; or, better still, to reshape the observations so that they may be perceived in a way that eliminates the discomfiture'.[5] Still, twenty years after Vernon's remarks, a good deal of analysis on technology growth and international trade has a 'reductionist' flavour, attempting more often than not to squeeze genuine dynamic problems of innovation, learning, uncertainty and change into the more familiar cloth of endowments, relative scarcities and optimization under budget constraints.

STRATEGIC TRADE THEORY AND TECHNICAL CHANGE

Recent 'new international economics'[6] have attempted to introduce some dynamic learning features associated with economies of scale and international rivalry. The policy conclusions emerging from this literature, particularly the theoretical support for infant industry support in a number of industries, has undoubtedly questioned much of the prevailing wisdom in trade policy. As Dixit pointed out in his contribution to Krugman's celebrated book on strategic trade policy: 'recent research contains support for almost all the vocal and popular views on trade policy that only a few years ago struggled against the economists' conventional wisdom of free trade. Now the mercantilist arguments for restricting imports and promoting exports are being justified on grounds of 'profit sharing'. The fears that other governments could capture permanent advantage in industry after industry by giving each industry a small initial impetus somewhere down the learning curve now emerges as the result of impeccable formal models. The claim that one's own government should be aggressive in the pursuit of such policies because other governments do the same is no longer dismissed as a non sequitur.'[7]

Such strategic trade theories have brought to the forefront many features which appear to be, at least at first sight, of particular relevance to the analysis of technical change and international trade. The importance of monopoly rents, of profit sharing and of strategic trade manipulation seem to be of particular relevance to many high-tech industries. Furthermore, the actual emergence of these new theories on the US academic scene occurred at a time of increasing fear in the USA of the Japanese trade and technology challenge.

While sympathetic to any attempt at introducing in trade theory some features of the 'imperfect' world we live in, it is difficult not to be very critical both of the way in which the technology factor has been introduced in such new trade theories and the simplistic policy recommendations which appear to emerge from the normative implications. The interpretation given to technology in the new trade vision is indeed only a poor reflection of the complexity of the process of technological change and innovation. It could be said that the simplicity of the way technological change is reduced to 'learning curves' in these recent trade theories is reflected in the simplicity of the policy recommendations of how to slide faster along such learning curve.

Process of technological change and innovation

In the next few pages we discuss, albeit briefly, some of the most characteristic features of technological change and innovation and as well as their implications for international trade flows. This leads us to the formulation of an alternative trade model based on some previous work and described in general terms in Section 3. Finally, we discuss in Section 4 some broad plans within the context of the further harmonization of the European Community's (EC's) internal market.

A more careful analysis of the process of technological change and innovation brings to the forefront a number of specific features some of which are more fundamentally at odds with the traditional economic view on 'technology'. First, technology in essence cannot be reduced to freely available information or to a set of 'blueprints'. Following some of the analyses of the process of technical change of Rosenberg, Nelson, Winter, Sahal, Freeman, Dosi and Pavitt, technology must be viewed as embodying specific, local, often tacit, and only partly appropriable knowledge. Each set of technical principles, search procedures, and forms of expertise – which Dosi has called 'technological paradigms' – would lead from this perspective to relatively ordered, cumulative and irreversible patterns of technical change: so-called 'technological trajectories'.

Paradigms and trajectories appear to differ in different sectors, according to the knowledge base on which they would draw, the strength of their linkages with pure science, the nature of the innovative search processes, the degrees of embodiment of technical advances in capital equipment and the forms of private appropriation of the economic benefits from innovation. On the basis of some of these indicators, Pavitt[8] has developed a sectoral taxonomy of the patterns of production and uses of innovation whereby significant differences in the contribution of each sector to the innovative output of the economic system could be identified.

Second, and as emphasized by Nelson[9] in particular, the widely accepted representation of 'technical progress' as a shift in the production function resulting from disembodied or embodied technical change does not adequately represent the more complex reality which emerges from a variety of industry and firm-based studies. It is a popular economic assumption to represent technology as exogenously generated and applicable either as information or as embodied in producer goods. However, in most sectors technology is generated endogenously.

Third, an important implication of such an analysis of technical change is the support for a *theory of production* whereby different ('better' and 'worse') techniques, products and firms coexist at any point in time. The main mechanism of change over time appears therefore to consist of an evolutionary process of innovation and diffusion of unequivocally better techniques and products.

Fourth, at the international level, such a view of technology can account for the continuous existence of technology gaps between firms and between countries, and for the conditions of *convergence* or *divergence* in inter-firm and international technological capabilities according to the degrees of opportunity cumulativeness and appropriability that each technology presents.

Fifth, from such a perspective, the degree of innovativeness of each country in any one particular technology is explained – with regards to its origin – through the complex inter-play between (*i*) science-related opportunities, (*ii*) country-specific and technology-specific institutions which foster or hinder the emergence of new technologies; and (*iii*) the nature and intensity of economic stimuli which stem from the abundance of particular inputs, or, alternatively, critical scarcities, specific patterns of demand and levels and changes in relative prices. The interpretation suggested accounts, in other words, for the evidence presented by some of the particular theories of 'market-induced' innovations (e.g. product-cycles, demand-pull, relative-price inducements) and incorporates such theories in a more general view of the innovative process.

Sixth, there is certainly a wide variety of economic inducements to innovation, but these belong to the necessary although not sufficient conditions. Sufficiency is provided by the degree of matching or mismatching that exists between these generic market opportunities and the institutional conditions related to the scientific/technological capabilities available in each country, the 'bridging institutions' between pure science and economic applications, the expertise embodied in the firm and the pattern of organization of the major markets.

Seventh, over time, capital accumulation and technological accumulation are interlinked so that improvements in input efficiencies and search or learning processes feed back to each other. In some respects, such an analysis overlaps with the question concerning 'why growth rates differ'. However, the interpretation is opposite to the traditional one: instead of explaining differences between countries in terms of differential endowments, the question is now 'how and why are such international differences related to the country-specific conditions of technological learning and accumulation?'

The implications of these and other discrepancies between traditional 'economic theory' assumptions and what could be viewed as the 'stylized' empirical reality have already been highlighted by many recent contributions to the economics of technological change. From a microeconomic perspective, a satisfactory theory will indeed have to be based on assumptions on the actual behaviours and characteristics of technology, innovation and competitive processes that can account for the prevailing observed behaviour at the level of the firm and the observed characteristics of the pattern of international trade.

In many ways, the emphasis of such a theory would be the opposite to the conventional one. Conventional trade theory, whether classical, neo-classical or 'new', has focused primarily on allocative optimality *for given techniques* and has consequently obscured the importance of differences in techniques and product characteristics between countries and neglected the analysis of their origin. It is quite evident, for example, that the wide international differences in per capita income stem primarily from the joint effect of differences in the degrees of capital accumulation and differences in technology rather than simply from differences in relative prices (or 'distortions' in the price mechanism).

Technology, trade and growth

The investigation of all these phenomena mentioned above developed separately from trade theories, which did not take technology gaps as one of the fundamental facts from which to start theorizing. This applies in different ways to both 'classical' and neo-classical theories. The latter excludes from the core of the model the implications of inferiority or superiority of techniques between countries for the validity of the most general theorems to hold, such as international factor price equalization. The former allows the existence of such international technological differences, but – as in the 'neo-Ricardian' re-formulations[10] – it takes a rather general and agnostic view, describing the equilibrium specializations irrespective of the nature of the techniques available in each country.

Elsewhere[11] we developed some hypotheses on the determinants of trade flows in those cases where techniques and product technologies can be univocally ranked, irrespective of domestic income distribution and relative prices. Technology gaps, we argued, are of paramount importance in determining the participation of each country to international trade flows and, through that, the maximum levels of income each country can attain, compatible with the foreign balance constraint. Some previous empirical results,[12] admittedly based on highly imperfect data, point to the dominance of a set of absolute advantages upon the factors pushing towards comparative advantages and specialization. In other words, the international composition of trade by countries within each sector appears to be explained essentially by technological gaps, while comparative advantage mechanisms appear to be of lesser importance.

In so far as technology gaps and their changes are a fundamental force in shaping international competitiveness, their impact on domestic income, by inducing and/or allowing relatively high rates of growth via the foreign trade multiplier, will be significant. However, the 'virtuous circle' between technological levels, foreign competitiveness and domestic growth is not entirely automatic and endogenous to the process of economic development. Country-specific and sector-specific innovative or imitative capabilities can be isolated as one of the single most important factors which originate these 'virtuous circles' and contribute to explanations of the patterns of international convergence or divergence in terms of trade performance, per capita incomes and rates of growth.

From such a perspective, it is the relationship between technology, trade and growth which is at the centre of the analysis, rather than the question about the short-term gains from trade stemming from the open-economy allocation of resources which is so crucial in the conventional view. The latter are indeed in their very nature 'once-and-for-all' gains: their dynamic relevance concerns the link between the 'static' pattern of allocation and the long-term performance of the economy. The empirical findings reported in Dosi, Pavitt and Soete (1990) are broadly consistent with the theoretical model. The most important conclusions can be summarized as follows:

1.   A variety of science and technology measures – R & D, patenting and innovation counts – gives a consistent picture of the aggregate international distribution of innovative activities among countries. Innovative activities are concentrated in relatively few countries. Although there have been significant changes since the beginning of this century in the relative importance of these countries, there has been only one major newcomer to the group, Japan.

2.   International differences in innovative activities are reflected in differences in shares of world exports in most sectors, and in manufacturing as a whole.

3.   Export performance is positively associated with differences in per capita innovative activities and differences in labour productivity.

4.   Changes in trade performance are more strongly associated with changes in innovative activities than changes in relative labour costs.

5.   Since the beginning of the century, international differences in per capita income have been closely related to international differences in per capita innovative activity. International differences in the rate of growth of per capita income have

been associated with similar differences in the rate of investment and in the rate of growth of innovative activities.

The evidence on the relationship between technological innovation and trade therefore demands a different theoretical representation, rather than an attempt at providing syntheses between traditional trade theory and specific partial features of the innovative process.

TOWARDS AN ALTERNATIVE MODEL OF TRADE, GROWTH AND TECHNOLOGY

It is impossible in these few pages to give a detailed account of what these insights on the innovative process sketched out above would imply as a starting point for the development of a model of trade based on the general existence of technological differences between countries. For this, the interested reader is referred to the detailed analysis of Dosi, Pavitt and Soete which is referred to above. Technological differences between countries are to some extent the equivalent of Smith's 'absolute advantages', but determine two fundamental processes of adjustments between, and within, countries.

First, inter-sectoral intra-national differences in technology gaps lead to a tendency towards relative specialization in the sectors of 'comparative advantages'. This is the familiar mechanism of adjustment described in the Ricardian (and, under different assumptions, in the neo-classical) literature.

Second, and at least as important, inter-sectoral gaps between countries would lead to adjustments in world market shares. This other adjustment process is closely related to the notion of 'absolute' or 'structural' competitiveness of each country. It is an 'absolute' notion in the sense that it does not relate to any inter-sectoral comparison ('I am relatively better in this or that'), although it obviously has a relative country content ('I am better or worse than country B or C').

Most of the trade literature nearly exclusively focuses upon the origins and effects of 'comparative advantages'. In the model we are thinking of revealed comparative advantages which to some extent are only a by-product of both intra-national, inter-sectoral changes in inputs allocations and, changes in the *absolute* amount of inputs each economy employs to produce for changing shares in the world market.

This analysis can easily be linked with a 'Keynesian' view of the determination of the rates of macroeconomic activity of each economy. Unlike pure neo-classical trade analysis – which generally imposes market-clearing conditions – and unlike Ricardian trade models – which generally assume steady-state growth – such a trade model allows, and indeed requires, changes in the level of macroeconomic activity of each economy in response to changes in international competitiveness. Thus, the link between absolute advantages and world market shares is theoretically consistent with a determination of domestic aggregate demand via the foreign trade multiplier. One can thus illustrate how international gaps in technology would define the boundaries of both 'Ricardian' processes of adjustment in specialization and 'Keynesian' adjustment in the rate of macroeconomic activity. From a dynamic point of view, it is the evolution in the innovative/imitative capabilities of each country which shapes the trend in the relative and absolute rates of growth of the tradable sector of each economy.

The normative implications of such an analysis are contrary to neo-classical or 'new' trade theory and are not straightforward. A discussion of normative issues, once out of the safe surroundings of market imperfections and anomalies, will indeed, as Nelson and Winter have warned: 'be complex and messy. It is unlikely that one will be able to prove many sweeping normative theorems of the sort that are now contained in our advanced treatises and elementary texts.'[13] The much more complex framework does not allow one to draw the sort of elegant recipes on 'Pareto optimality' of standard trade analysis. The complexity of the innovative process, the multiplicity of adjustment mechanisms and the variety of institutional frameworks can hardly be judged on simple and immutable yardsticks.

However, the theoretical approach sketched out above does allow for a normative counterpart. It is possible to identify some general conditions under which conflicts between 'allocative' (which we will call 'Ricardian') efficiency and 'dynamic' efficiency (related to innovative and demand dynamism) could arise.

A first question regards the effect that the pattern of allocation – pulled by comparative advantages (and, thus, relative inter-sectoral profitabilities) on the basis of given technologies – will have on technological dynamism and long-term macroeconomic rates of activity. One can call the performance criterion related to innovative dynamism 'Schumpeterian efficiency' and that related to the maximum rate of growth consistent with the foreign balance constraint 'growth' or 'Keynesian' efficiency.

There appears to be nothing in the mechanism leading to 'Ricardian' efficiency that would also guarantee the fulfilment of the other criteria of efficiency. The easiest way to see the efficiency gains in a Ricardian world is to imagine that each nation, before trade, operates at full employment rates of activity and that there are no Keynesian adjustment processes linking absolute advantages, market shares and macroeconomics rates of activity in the transition from autarchy to trade.[14] With all the other restrictive assumptions, one can easily see the full operation of the theorem of comparative advantage: each trading partner gains from trade since it gets more commodities of a certain kind from abroad than it would otherwise be able to manufacture domestically without forgoing any production and consumption of the commodities in which it specializes. It can also be seen how gains from trade of this kind are of a 'once-and-for-all', static nature.

Let us now relax both assumptions and ask what the effect of any given pattern of specialization might be upon the dynamics of the technological capabilities of each country, and what the outcome would be, in the short and long run, in terms of macroeconomic rates of activities whenever one allows for 'Keynesian' adjustments. It might be useful to recall the cumulative, (partly) appropriable and local nature of technological advances; the widespread existence of static and dynamic economies of scale; the influence that technological gaps between firms and between countries have upon the economic signals agents face; and the importance of country-specific and area-specific untraded interdependencies. These factors taken together allow for the possibility of significant trade-offs between statics and dynamics. If different commodities or sectors present significant differences in their 'dynamic potential' (in terms of economies of scale, technical progress, possibilities of division of labour, learning-by-doing, etc.), specializations which are efficient in terms of comparisons of given sets of input coefficients may either generate in the long run virtuous or vicious circles of technological backwardness.

This is more than a special case related to infant industries: it is the general condition of an economic system whereby technological opportunities vary across products and across sectors. Within each technology and each sector, the technological capabilities of each firm and each country are associated with the actual process of production and innovation in the area. Thus, the mechanisms regarding international specialization have a dynamic effect in that they also select the areas where technical skills will be accumulated, (possibly) innovation undertaken, economies of scale reaped and so on. However, the potential for these effects is widely different between technologies and sectors. This is another aspect of the irreversibility feature of economic processes: present allocative choices influence the direction and rate of the future evolution of technological coefficients. Whenever we abandon the idea of technology as a set of blueprints and we conceive of technical progress as joint production with manufacturing, it is possible to imagine an economic system which is dynamically better off (in terms of productivity, innovativeness, etc.) if it evolves in disequilibrium *vis-à-vis* Ricardian conditions of allocative efficiency than otherwise.

It is rather easy to see how a trade-off between 'allocative efficiency' and 'Schumpeterian efficiency' can emerge. The patterns of specialization (with their properties of Ricardian efficiency) are determined, for each country, by the relative size of the sector-specific technology gaps (or leads). Whenever the gap is highest in the most dynamic technologies (i.e. those characterized by the highest technological opportunities), allocative efficiency will conflict directly with Schumpeterian efficiency.

CONCLUSION

We would suggest that the likelihood of such trade-offs between Ricardian and Schumpeterian efficiencies is proportional to the distance of each country from the technological frontier in the newest, most dynamic and most pervasive technologies.

Technological leaders will tend to find the pattern of their inter-sectoral profitability signals pointing in the direction of activities which also lead to the highest demand growth and the highest potential of future product and process innovations. Conversely, countries well behind the technological frontier may be 'dynamically penalized' by their present pattern of inter-sectoral allocative efficiency. This property contributes, to the relative stability of the 'pecking order' between countries in terms of technological innovativeness and interactional competitiveness, and the relatively ordered ways in which this 'pecking order' changes in the long term. The interactions between present economic signals, patterns of specialization and dynamics of the sectoral technology gaps provides the ground of cumulative processes.

Major changes in the interactional distribution of innovative activities and in the international competitiveness of each economy can, however, be associated with the emergence of new technological paradigms. This occurrence re-shapes the pattern of technological advantages or disadvantages between countries, often demands different organizational and institutional set-ups and sometimes presents a unique 'window of opportunity' (in Perez and Soete's words)[15] for the emergence of new technological and economic leaders.

The foregoing arguments can be summarized in the following way. Markets characterized by decentralized decision-making fulfil two fundamental functions. First, they provide a mechanism of co-ordination between individual economic decisions and, in doing so, they reallocate resources in ways which – under the conditions specified by the theory – present properties of efficiency. Second, whenever one allows technological progress to take place (with its features of search, uncertainty, etc.), markets provide an incentive to innovate through the possibility of private appropriation of some economic benefit stemming from technical progress itself.

As soon as these second functions of markets are taken into account in the theoretical picture, their efficiency properties become blurred and complicated to assess, even in a closed economy context: allocative efficiency in a static sense may conflict with dynamic efficiency in terms of incentives to technological progress. Overlapping with the 'Schumpeterian trade-off' of the closed-economy case, there is the possibility of a static versus dynamic trade-off originating from the pattern of economic signals in the international market. In a way, the open economy case induces a structural distortion on that pattern of signals which would have been generated under autarchy conditions. In doing so, they may either overrule the domestic 'Schumpeterian trade-offs' or amplify them. The hypothesis we suggested above is that this depends on the relative distance of each country *vis-à-vis* the technological frontier in those technological paradigms showing the highest opportunities of innovation and demand growth.

Any judgement on the regime of trade which should have preference should therefore also take into account an evaluation of the relationship between technological gaps, market signals and conditions of technological accumulation under the different regimes.

Policy implications in the context of Europe 1992

It seems appropriate to conclude this introductory chapter with a couple of reflections on the technology trade relationship within the context of the completion by the end of 1992 of the large European internal market. For most EC member countries, this represents – both in its scale and scope – one of the major structural changes of the post-war period. 'Nineteen ninety-two' means less a change in absolute macroeconomic output and employment growth potential than a change in the potential for structural change: it implies a significant rationalization and increased efficiency potential resulting from the opening up of all sectors to intra-EC competition; it will see a significantly increased potential for labour, skill and capital mobility; and it presents the possibility of significant shifts in the location of regional growth. In terms of the potential for structural transformation, the nature and size of Europe's internal market completion is historically unprecedented.

The opening up to free trade or at least the harmonization of the large internal European market is likely to provide a major impetus to more rapid use and application of technological change, particularly in regions and sectors which have been at the periphery of the traditional European growth poles. It brings to the forefront in our previous analysis the importance of catching up, and possibly even shifts in technological competitiveness towards regions which possess both certain comparative cost advantages and benefit at the same time from certain minimum absolute cost advantages in terms, for example, of the right set of available infrastructure, educational provisions and institutional back-up. As a case in point one can think of Southern Europe and, in particular, of Spain and Portugal.

The specific EC market completion feature adds, indeed, three important dimensions to the traditional trade technology debate. First, the process of convergence likely to be set in motion as a result of the further harmonization of the internal EC market will in all likelihood lead to more rapid growth and more rapid diffusion of new technologies in catching-up countries or regions. In other words, there will probably be an increase in the variation in economic growth as between member countries and, as a consequence, also shifts in growth poles within the EC.

Second, and by the same token, some of the more 'mature' countries or regions, having benefited most from the liberalization and gains from trade in the 1960s and 1970s, will have a more specialized industrial structure, possibly more vulnerable to the further diffusion of, for example, new information technologies. This will depend fundamentally on the existing specialization structure. For some countries and regions this might amount to a reinforcing impact on a structure very much in line with such technologies; for others the opposite might be true. In so far as the international dimension is the logical extension of the regional dimension, the issue of the *spatial* impact of technological change within a large free trade zone is here the central point of analysis.

Third, the implications of this process of growth polarization for 'national' or regional employment growth and skill shortages are fundamental. On the one hand, because of intra-EC labour mobility, 'national' skill shortages or employment displacement might lose some of their meaning in favour of broad estimates at the supra-national EC level. On the other hand, local skill shortages and employment displacement become, even more clearly than before, major bottlenecks for the rapid diffusion and application of new technologies and the emergence of new growth poles. The likely structural adjustment impact of the harmonization of the internal European market, and its possible 'accelerating' impact on the diffusion of new technologies, adds in other words an interesting 'new' dimension to strategic 'national' trade or industrial policy.

Reaping the benefits and advantages from technological change and the further harmonization of the internal EC market is a crucial national challenge for each individual nation, with significant implications for its international competitiveness; though the scope for doing so through traditional national industrial policy means will have by and large disappeared. What emerges as far more crucial though is the establishment and maintenance at the regional level of a sufficient level of 'absolute' advantage conditions both in terms of educational and the wide variety of infrastructural provisions.

3 Technology, trade policy and Schumpeterian efficiencies

Giovanni Dosi, John Zysman and Laura D'Andrea Tyson

INTRODUCTION: US ECONOMIC PERFORMANCE AND COMPETITIVENESS

The growing debate on free trade and US competitiveness has focused attention on manufacturing capacity, innovation and international performance.[1] The scale and composition of the trade deficits of the past few years are among the most prominent indicators that the competitive position of the US economy is weakening.[2] They reveal that the trajectory of technological development that carried the US to industrial dominance in the past is being challenged by a paradigm that has put some of our most important competitors on distinctive technological trajectories. If the position which we outline in this chapter (and collectively, in this book) is correct, then traditional economic frameworks cannot explain or reverse the decline in the USA's position in the international economy nor can they help us compete in an era of expanded liberal trade.

The huge trade deficits of the 1980s were driven by sharp increases in the value of the dollar that priced US goods out of world markets and made imports a bargain. The inflow of funds to finance the budget deficits pushed the exchange rate up. Consequently, some economists argue, the problem is fundamentally one of mistaken domestic macroeconomic policy. The process that created the trade deficits is reversible: reduce the budget deficit, thereby reducing demand for foreign borrowings to finance it; thereby reduce the trade deficit. To us, however, this established view is built on a static equilibrium perspective of traditional trade theory. It is not so much wrong as it is limited and limiting.

Fifteen years ago, the traditional remedy suggested by traditional theory seemed to work: currency devaluation rapidly reversed trade flows. This time, however, it has not, at least not as expected. Since 1985, the US dollar has lost about half its value against the yen, but the trade deficit has stubbornly refused to follow suit. Only at the end of 1987 was a monthly decline first registered: the deficit fell to $13 billion, which itself had been a record just a few months earlier. Certainly there is some price for the dollar at which imports would dry up and exports explode – if people had confidence that the exchange rate advantage would last. But balancing our external trade account is not the only objective. All nations, even the poorest, eventually do this. The trick is to do it with high and rising incomes: this is the definition of national competitiveness.[3] A permanently falling dollar translates into an increasingly impoverished USA.

Certainly, the USA has many new competitors. Two of the most important are Japan and Europe. Japan's trade pattern is different from those of other advanced economies for which intra-sectoral trade has been the key to open trade. Indeed, from a traditional analytic perspective, Japan has done many things 'wrong'. During the first two decades of its post-war development, perhaps longer, Japanese markets were formally closed to the penetration of foreign goods and capital. The Ministry of Trade and Industry (MITI), with the help of the Ministry of Finance and other government organizations, effectively acted as a gatekeeper to the Japanese market, limiting the access of foreigners and targeting industries and firms for promotional policies.[4] Capacity expansions and reductions in particular industries were often planned on a firm-by-firm basis, and numerous and growing violations of Japan's anti-trust law were left unchecked. Cartels and other information mechanisms for market sharing and risk sharing among domestic producers were overlooked or actively encouraged by Japanese policy-makers convinced that, under certain conditions, 'controlled' competition was preferable to market competition. Foreign direct investment was precluded, and the import of foreign technology was strictly controlled by MITI, which acted as an intermediary between domestic firms and foreign suppliers of technology, often to the benefit of the former and the disadvantage of the latter. Interest rates were held below market clearing levels, and credit was allocated to targeted firms and activities at preferential rates, while non-priority borrowers were credit constrained. Exports were promoted not by simple reliance on the 'correct' exchange rate but by a variety of tax, credit and protectionist policies that raised the returns to exports to Japanese producers. In targeting industries for preferential policy, Japanese policy-makers explicitly overrode notions of comparative advantage in favour of such ill-defined criteria as the dynamic or technological potential of a particular economic activity.[5]

Today, policies like those adopted in Japan are routinely attacked by the International Monetary Fund (IMF) and the World Bank, the two most influential international organizations advising countries on development strategy.[6] Few would deny, however, that Japan has been a spectacular success story in economic development.

In the Japanese variant of capitalism, markets have been emphasized as a source of growth rather than as a source of short-run efficiency, and a primary role of government has been to supply incentives to promote growth through markets. The perspective motivating Japanese policy has been explicitly dynamic and explicitly developmental. Japanese policy-makers have chosen to target industries for promotion on the basis of their perceived potential for economic growth and technological change. In the words of this analysis, they have emphasized long-term growth and 'Schumpeterian efficiencies' over short-run or 'Ricardian efficiency' in their choice of industrial targets. Their targeting strategy has had long-term beneficial effects on the competitive position of Japanese producers in a variety of critical industrial sectors in world markets. To understand these effects, it is necessary to abandon the static assumptions of international trade theory, even the so-called 'new' trade theory, and to adopt a dynamic model in which national patterns of production and trade specialization at a moment in time can affect a nation's growth and technological trajectory.

Today Japan appears to be opening up a new 'technology gap' over its major industrial competitors. It has developed a new technology system based on a cluster of new transformative technologies and a new approach to using them. The evidence suggests that the world is at the beginning of something akin to a third Industrial Revolution based on the productive capabilities of these new technologies, and that Japan is at the forefront of developing and using them to competitive advantage in a variety of sectors. In contrast to the protective policies and mass production strategies that were characteristic of the second Industrial Revolution, the new revolution will, of necessity, feature freer trade and flexibility in both production organization and technology-sourcing strategies (see David Teece's argument in this volume).

These experiences – plus the emerging orientation towards free trade – strongly attest to the need to reconsider traditional notions of the appropriate role of government policy and markets in economic development and to examine alternative institutional forms of capitalism. The 'US' model of capitalism, which is the model which permeates traditional thought on technology, economics and trade, is clearly not the only model of capitalism nor does it appear to be the most promising one from a developmental point of view. Laying the groundwork for this reconsideration is the purpose of this chapter.

TECHNOLOGY, TRADE AND POLICY

Traditional trade theory

Until the late 1970s, international trade theory was dominated by the concept of comparative advantage. Intuitively, this concept implies that nations trade in order to take advantage of differences in their productive capabilities. More formally, it implies that countries tend to export in sectors in which they have a comparative production advantage relative to their competitors and to import in sectors in which they have a comparative production disadvantage. According to the theory of comparative advantage, even a country with an absolute production disadvantage, in the sense of higher domestic costs of production for all traded commodities, gains from trade by exporting those goods in which its production disadvantage is least.

In formal standard models of comparative advantage, production is assumed to exhibit constant returns to scale.[7] Both increasing returns in the traditional sense and learning curve economies are excluded. Markets for tradeable products are assumed to be perfectly competitive, and trade is assumed to occur under full employment conditions. Under these assumptions, trade arises only to the extent that countries differ in tastes, technology or factor endowments. Ricardian models of trade explain comparative advantage in terms of a single key factor of production, such as labour productivity or natural resource endowments, or in terms of technological differences. The Heckscher–Ohlin variant of comparative advantage theory assumes the existence of two or more factors of production –

usually labour and capital – and argues that countries will tend to export goods embodying their relatively abundant factors and to the cost economies of increased scale of production while maintaining or increasing the diversity of goods available. In addition, trade may actually reduce the market imperfections that would be associated with a closed economy by subjecting producers to more competition in world markets with a larger number of competing producers. Thus the new models seem to confirm the welfare implications of the more standard models: trade is a good thing with mutual gains for all.

A closer look at this argument, though, shows that with increasing returns and imperfect competition, free trade is not necessarily and automatically the best policy. Trade without barriers and government policies of promotion that distort markets may improve national welfare. However, government policy to strengthen the competitive position of domestic producers in world markets may generate higher levels of national welfare than would result from free trade.

In recent years, the 'new' trade theory literature has concentrated on conditions under which government policy of intervention and promotion may actually improve national welfare. There are essentially two different types of conditions that give rise to this result. First, industries that are imperfectly competitive tend to generate high returns (excess profits or quasi-rents) – in other words, the resources employed by these sectors earn higher returns than those available in the rest of the economy. Under these conditions, national welfare may be improved by government policy to win larger share of world profits for the domestic population. If the world computer industry is a high-profit, high-wage industry, then national protectionist and promotional policies that capture a large share of the world computer industry for domestic producers and workers may improve national welfare at the expense of competitors abroad.

As is obvious from this example, such policies act to shift the world pool of returns in a particular high-return industry from one set of national producers to another and are thus inherently 'beggar-thy-neighbour' type policies. The new trade theory literature often refers to this rationale for government policy as a 'profit/rip-off' rationale. National policies that target the successful high-return, export industries of other nations for development are sometimes understood from this vantage point.

Government policies to improve national industrial welfare can be justified by a second set of conditions. Standard notions of externalities or spillover effects define these conditions. Simply put, certain industries may be more important than others because they generate benefits for the rest of the economy, and government policies to promote or protect them can improve welfare by fostering these spillover effects. In fact, the proposition that protectionist or promotional policies can improve national welfare when an industry generates external economies is part of the conventional theory of trade policy. In a sense there is nothing really new about this branch of the new trade theory. What the new literature has done is to strengthen the case for welfare-improving policy by focusing on externalities resulting from the research and development activities of high-tech industries and by linking the analysis of externalities to the analysis of the imperfectly competitive market conditions inherently characteristic of such industries.[8]

High-tech industries are likely to generate positive externalites because of the knowledge generated by their R&D activities and because the benefits of this knowledge cannot be completely appropriated by the private agents who pay the costs for the generation of such knowledge. It is useful to distinguish three different kinds of knowledge generated by R&D and innovation:

1.   knowledge, such as production process knowledge reflected in firm-specific learning curves, that can be internalized within a firm and is therefore largely appropriable;

2.   knowledge of product design that once generated can often be captured by competitors through reverse-engineering exercises; and

3.   knowledge which spreads beyond the innovating firm but not necessarily easily beyond national or sometimes even regional boundaries.[9]

This third kind of knowledge is often embodied in people and spread through social and academic networks. Both the second and third kinds of knowledge generate benefits that are not completely appropriable by the innovating agent. In industries experiencing rapid technological progress, firms routinely take each other's products apart to see how they work and how they are made and (at least in the USA) firms routinely 'raid' one another's R&D talent in order to secure the knowledge which they embody. The third kind of knowledge may be largely appropriable within a given set of national or regional boundaries, but not by the agents responsible for footing the R&D bill that gave rise to the knowledge.

When knowledge is not completely appropriable, the social returns to R&D investment activities are likely to exceed the private returns. This is the standard externality argument in support of policies to promote improvement in national economic welfare.[10] It applies equally both to domestic industries and to those involved in international trade. As long as the externalities resulting from such policies are international in scope − in other words, as long as the knowledge fostered by such policies flows across national boundaries as easily as within them − then each nation stands to benefit from the policies of its trading partners. A technological breakthrough sponsored by government policy in Japan or Europe, for example, can benefit US producers just as it benefits Japanese and European producers. The bottom line is that the resulting knowledge has the potential to benefit everyone regardless of national boundaries.

In contrast, there is a potential conflict of interest if knowledge spills over within a country but not between countries. Such conflict of interest in the support of high-tech industries becomes even more pronounced once one recognizes that such industries are never perfectly competitive. Investment in knowledge inevitably has a fixed-cost component: once a firm has improved its product or technique the unit cost of that improvement falls as more is produced. The result is dynamic economies of scale that undermine perfect competition and eliminate a basic premise of the free trade argument. Indeed, since each piece of new knowledge must be different from previously produced knowledge, the assumption of homogeneous products on which perfect competition rests must be largely invalid for markets based on technological competition. Under these circumstances, government policies that promote the R&D activities of high-tech industries may win a larger share of the world returns from such industries for domestic producers and workers and at the same generate externalities primarily for domestic producers and only secondarily for foreign ones.

In other words, both 'profit/rip-off' and external rationales for policies to target high-tech industries may exist in particular circumstances. As an illustration, a targeting policy to promote the Japanese computer industry may generate technological knowledge from which both Japanese and US firms may benefit, but the policy may also increase the share of the Japanese producers in world production and returns at the expense of the share of US producers.

The new trade theory literature provides theoretical conditions under which government policies to promote particular industries or activities because of their strategic characteristics can improve national economic welfare relative to the free trade outcome. This conclusion has provoked some heated debates among economists about the wisdom of such policies.[11] First, there is a debate about the feasibility of evaluating whether an industry is strategic or not − how does one measure the extent of increasing returns and the nature of imperfect competition or the extent of externalities? Even with the most sophisticated tools currently at our disposal, such measures are empirically very difficult and subject to large errors.[12] Second, there is a debate about how one evaluates whether a proposed policy will do more harm than good, especially when its effects on other industries or activities not targeted by policy are considered. Uncertainty is a feature of all economic policy but it becomes even more important when the key issue is how a policy will affect firms in an imperfectly competitive industry. For example, as Krugman notes, the effects of a protectionist trade policy or an R&D subsidy depend crucially on whether firms behave co-operatively or non-cooperatively, whether they compete by setting prices or outputs, whether there is a sort of 'winner takes all' game, or conversely, whether benefits of research strategies are shared also by competitors.[13]

Unfortunately, it is both theoretically and empirically difficult to predict which form of behaviour is most likely. If, as many models indicate, the effects of an interventionist policy is to encourage non-cooperative behaviour and the entry of new firms, then the national benefits of intervention may be dissipated by competition which drives excess profits to zero in the world market or which passes the benefits of national R&D policies to foreign consumers in the form or lower prices. Furthermore, to determine whether strategic policy is welfare-improving or not, the government must understand its effects not only on the targeted industry, which is difficult enough, but also on other industries.

Finally, there is a debate among economists about how widespread and important are strategic activities. If one believes that competition in world industries rapidly drives excess profits to zero, that learning spreads quickly and costlessly across firms and countries and that market prices are good indicators of social returns both now and in the future, then there are few strategic activities that can benefit from market-promoting policies. If, instead, one believes that large excess profits in particular industries or activities can persist for long periods of time despite competition and that prices are poor indicators of social returns now or in the future, then the scope for welfare-improving policies can be quite broad. As the chapters in this book indicate, it was the latter perspective that motivated Japanese developmental policy during the post-war period, while the former perspective is clearly the basis of policy-making in the USA.

Revisionist trade theory

The new trade theory pushes the limits of traditional economic thought concerning the welfare effects of government policy but it still reflects many of the assumptions and foundations of such thought. In particular, the new trade theory is inherently static in its orientation. It is centrally concerned with the problem of the optimal allocation of existing resources. Its models examine the once-and-for-all gains that may be obtained by different patterns of resource allocation, a market-determined one and a policy-driven one. Typically, these models show that under certain stringent conditions, a policy-induced outcome may induce a once-and-for-all improvement in economic welfare, due in the last resort to better terms of trade which the domestic economy enjoys with the help of policy.

The rationale behind Japanese developmental policy, for example, has different intellectual roots. Japanese policy-makers have been critically concerned about *the links between current resource allocation decisions and the future evolution of the economy.* In the words of one MITI official: '... optimal resource allocation from a long-term dynamical viewpoint cannot be accomplished by the market mechanism alone ... this is an area in which industrial policy can – and should – play a useful role.[14] It is this perspective which led Japanese officials to abandon the theory of comparative advantage as a guide to policy and to target industries and technologies which in their view had the greatest potential to promote rapid economic growth and development over time. It is impossible to understand this perspective within the confines of the new trade theory. An inherently dynamic analytical framework is needed, and we attempt to develop one here.

Our starting point in this chapter is to draw a distinction between what we call 'Ricardian' or 'allocative' efficiency, on the one hand, and 'growth' or 'Schumpeterian' efficiency, on the other. The allocation of resources amongst industries and activities in response to current measures of social profitability is 'Ricardian' efficient, in the sense that it maximizes current economic welfare. In the case of market imperfections and externalities of the types discussed above, the realization of 'Ricardian' efficiency may require government intervention. It should also be noted that in the presence of increasing returns, there are in theory many possible points of 'Ricardian' efficiency – multiple outcomes are possible and which outcomes are realized depends in part on government policy.

As an illustration, consider two countries which each can undertake production in two possible industries – let us say, aircraft and computers – each of which has large set-up costs or some other source of increasing returns.[15] Given current market conditions, a possible 'Ricardian' efficient arrangement would be for one country to produce all of one commodity, earning the returns for its domestic population, the other to produce all of the other. The countries could then trade in order to arrive at their preferred consumption mix to the benefit of both.

There are, however, two possible arrangements. Which commodity is produced in which country is indeterminate. And when the two countries differ in size or the two industries differ in their potential for future demand growth or future technological change, the two possible outcomes can have different welfare consequences in both the short run and the long run. Furthermore, the outcome will be sensitive to the initial conditions of competition between the two countries.

More concretely, the early history of market shares – in part the consequence of past government policy – can determine which solution ultimately prevails, that is, which country produces what. In short, with increasing returns and imperfect competition, market outcomes which are 'Ricardian' efficient in the sense that they maximize current economic welfare are themselves path-dependent – history as well as contemporary indicators of social profitability affect the outcome.

The allocation of resources amongst industries and activities can be evaluated not only according to its Ricardian efficiency but also according to two other performance criteria: its growth efficiency, or its effects on long-term rates of growth of economics activity; and its Schumpeterian efficiency, or its effects on the pace and direction of technological change. These two criteria clearly have dominated Japanese economic policy-making in a self-conscious way. As Freeman argues in his insightful book on Japanese technology policy, 'MITI saw as one of its key functions the promotion of the most advanced technologies with the widest world market potential in the long run.'[16]

In the following discussion, we will examine notions of growth efficiency and technological efficiency in greater detail, and we will explain why – under conditions of imperfect competition and technological change – an allocation of resources which is efficient by current market indicators (i.e. efficiency in the Ricardian sense) may not be efficient in the Schumpeterian sense.

TECHNOLOGICAL DEVELOPMENT AND GROWTH

Equilibria and trajectories

As Patel and Pavitt articulate in this book, a nation's future growth and technological development is affected by the current composition of its industries and activities by its current allocation of resources, and by its paradigms of how to develop and exploit technology. As a result of its economic history, each country must be understood to be on a distinct developmental trajectory.

If the dynamic potential of economic activities differs, then a national specialization at a given moment, which is efficient in terms of a given set of market indicators, may not maximize economic welfare in the long run. If private agents and policy-makers allocate resources according to these indicators, the future development trajectory of the economy may be adversely affected. A nation may realize an efficient allocation of resources to specialize in those industries and activities in which the opportunities for growth and technological development are least. In this case there can be a real conflict between short-term Ricardian efficiency and longer term dynamic efficiency.

A consequence of this perspective is that the outcome of strategic trade conflicts which are likely to emerge within increasingly free trade environments is not simply a matter of the one-time gains or losses that result when one government's policy allows its firms to gain a dominant position in global markets to the disadvantage of its trading partners. What is at stake are future gains and losses in terms of each nation's dynamic potential. A nation's current competitive successes and failures in international trade will affect the areas in which it will be able to accumulate technical skills, innovate and foster diversified but well-integrated economies of scale. To understand the notion for strategic purposes in this dynamic sense, it is necessary to consider in more detail the ideas of growth efficiency and technological efficiency.

Growth efficiency and development trajectories

The idea of growth efficiency is essentially demand-sided. It rests fundamentally on a Keynesian assumption that an economy's growth depends on the growth of demand for its products. This assumption, in turn, rests on the implicit assumption that there are always unutilized resources that can be mobilized to meet growing demand. In other words, economic growth is primarily constrained by demand growth, not by supply capabilities. This is likely to be the reality in most modern economies. These theories assume the aggregate level and rate of growth of economic activity to be unaffected by trade. The growth efficiency idea, in contrast, considers how trade outcomes may affect growth over time by influencing patterns of national specialization. Countries may specialize, as a result of trade, in industries with different growth potential in world markets.

When the world is a Keynesian one, the growth efficiency of a particular pattern of production and trade specialization depends in part on the income elasticities of demand for different products in world markets – or, in other words, on how fast the demand for particular products increases as world income grows. Intuitively, the idea is that the faster the demand for a nation's products increases in world markets the faster the demand for a nation's products increases in world markets as world income grows, the faster that economy will be able to grow, all other things being equal. Since products differ significantly in their income elasticities, a pattern of specialization in goods with high income elasticities of demand generates more rapid growth prospects for a nation's products in world markets and is therefore superior according to the growth efficiency criterion. Seen from this perspective, other things being equal, a nation with a large percentage of its output and exports in apparel, a product with a low income elasticity of demand, has less attractive long-run growth prospects than a nation with a large percentage of its output and exports in telecommunications equipment, a product with a high income elasticity of demand. It is exactly this kind of thinking that led the Japanese to target industries whose products were perceived to have high income elasticities as a foundation for rapid economic growth. Similar choices have been adopted and defended by a variety of developing countries around the world.

Economists tend to attack this kind of reasoning because it overlooks the role of relative prices in the demand for a nation's exports in world markets. A nation may be highly specialized in the production and export of foods with low growth potential on the income side. None the less, if the relative prices of its products fall over time, demand for its goods can continue to grow rapidly. Actually, this argument has two parts. First, if the relative price of the goods produced by the nation falls in world markets over time, world demand might shift towards such products as a result of price-driven substitution in world consumption patterns. This first line of reasoning rests on the assumptions that the price elasticities of demand for traded products in world markets are relatively large and that the possibilities of price-related substitution in consumption are quite broad. Given what we know about patterns of world demand, these are questionable assumptions. Second, even if the pattern of world demand does not change, a nation may win a growing share of a declining world market, if it becomes a more price competitive producer in that market, either through devaluation or through other cost-cutting means. This line of reasoning implies that a nation's Ricardian allocation would necessarily be optimal for long run growth potential.

Why might current market signals fail to yield an allocation of resources that maximizes an economy's growth potential? One possibility, of course, is the existence of capital market imperfections or constraints. Firms or would-be entrepreneurs may be able to raise funds for investments in industries that offer high rates of returns over relatively short periods of time but be unable to raise funds for investment in industries which offer returns that are both uncertain, given existing world market conditions, and recoverable only over the long run. If national capital markets are 'impatient' and risk averse, then it may be difficult to invest in risky, long-term projects despite their long-term growth potential.

Imperfect product markets, moreover, make it impossible to reconcile fully the future risks and returns on current investment in uncertain and emerging industries and technologies. Under conditions of non-decreasing returns there is simply no way that markets can relate the varying future growth efficiencies of various industries to relative profitability signals facing individual producers. Basically, this argument is a variant of the infant industry argument. Because of increasing returns, current market signals can be misleading indicators of future profitability. Consequently, government policies to promote a domestic industry with high future growth potential can improve economic welfare over the long run. Without such policies, producers may well find it profitable to produce goods which a decreasing number of people on world markets may want to buy. The reader may think as extreme examples of the growth consequences of patterns of short-run specialization in such 'inferior' products as jute, mechanical typewriters, or black and white televisions, as compared to the growth consequences of specialization in such income-dynamic products as synthetic fibre, word processors and colour televisions. As this analysis makes clear, limited price-induced substitution between products and patterns of demand that are largely determined by product-specific income elasticities may well imply a painful trade-off between short-term allocations of resources that are Ricardian efficient and those patterns of production which could yield comparatively higher rates of macroeconomic growth.

As a resource-poor country, Japan's growth potential was seen by Japanese planners to be constrained by its ability to sustain high imports of resources over time. Under these circumstances, Japan needed to develop a production base that could generate huge exports of industrial products over time without requiring declines in Japan's terms of trade. Products which appeared to have high income elasticities of demand in world markets seemed to be the most promising avenue of development over the long run. Yet at any moment in time, given current world market conditions, Japanese producers might have found it more profitable to allocate resources to other products which were efficient in the Ricardian sense. If the markets for all products were perfectly competitive, a condition not realized because of the prevalence of increasing returns in many industries – especially those with high income elasticities of demand in world trade – then producers would have been able to move easily from one line of production to others as the growth potential of different products changed over time. As it was, a decision not to develop an industry with high growth potential at a given moment of time was not easily reversible. Failure to break into a high growth potential product at one point in time increased the costs of doing so at a later date.

Before leaving this discussion of growth efficiencies, it is important to note one additional way in which the composition of a nation's output can affect its potential for growth over time. As the new trade theorists have pointed out, imperfectly competitive industries can generate excess returns, and government policy can influence the distribution of these returns among countries. In static models, policies to win a larger national share of world returns in such industries have a once-and-for-all effect on national income and welfare. But if higher returns today finance higher national investment rates and more R&D, there may be dynamic effects as well. Such effects may be particularly important in high-tech industries. While investments in physical capital goods are often financed by borrowing, using the physical capital as collateral, expenditures on R&D are not for the most part collateralizable investments.[17] If firms confront difficulties in raising external capital to finance their R&D investment, then their R&D activities may be constrained by their current returns, and higher returns resulting from a targeted government policy may result in a higher R&D effort to improve their competitive position tomorrow. This insight may explain in part why Japanese semiconductor firms were able to mount a huge R&D and investment drive in the late 1970s while the efforts of their US competitors pale by comparison. As the Japanese firms captured a growing share of the world market from US producers and as the profit margins of Japanese firms were bolstered by the dramatic appreciation of the dollar, Japanese producers were able to finance massive R&D investments in both process and product innovations that allowed them to surpass the technological levels of their US competitors. Meanwhile, US firms with declining profits and even losses in some cases were unable to raise sufficient internal and external funds to mount a sustained R&D response to the growing Japanese challenge.

The idea that the excess returns resulting from a strong opposition in a high-tech industry may affect the technological dynamism of that industry over time goes back to Schumpeter. According to Schumpeter,[18] the dynamism of capitalism depends largely on competition based on new products and processes rather than on price competition. And competition in new products and processes both results in and depends on imperfect competition. Without the lure of excess returns, there will be no incentive to innovate, and with innovation and the market imperfections it creates the excess profits required as an incentive to innovate will exist. Although Schumpeter made his arguments at the industry level, they can be applied to the national level as well. Nations which support the competitive success of their high-tech industries in world markets can strengthen the incentives to innovate by domestic producers. The results may be greater technological dynamism and more rapid economic growth over the long run.

Development trajectories and technological dynamics: the meaning of 'Schumpeterian efficiency'

Economic development is fundamentally a product of technological change. To understand different national development trajectories, we need to understand the process of technological change. Yet traditional economic models provide little help in understanding this process.

Formal economic theory treats technology as unchanging. Or, more precisely, the ways in which technology changes are conceived as largely independent of the current allocation of resources. In this sense, technological change is largely exogenous to economic models and analysis. Traditional studies of economic growth, for example, usually find that a significant share of total growth is attributable to technological development, but they treat the technology component of growth as exogenous or unexplained.[19] If technology is a central determinant of growth, however, how can we have a theory of growth without a theory of technological change?

A quite different view emerges from studies of the process and history of technical change. These studies indicate that technology is not a set of blueprints given by scientific advances that occur independently of the production process but often a joint output of the production process itself.[20] The pace and direction of technological innovation and diffusion are shaped by production and market position. Technological knowledge is not simply information that can be bought or sold, but often a subtler set of insights that develop only in conjunction with production. From this perspective, technological knowledge is not disembodied knowledge that can be purchased like a pattern for a sweater or a supercomputer but rather it is rooted in the activities of design and production.

An obvious implication is that different mixes of production today mean different technological opportunities and different technological capabilities tomorrow. According to this view, within each technology and each sector the technological capabilities of firms and countries are generally associated with the actual process of production in the same or closely related activities. The pattern of technological change is not exogenous but is shaped by current patterns of resource allocation and production.

Moreover, at any moment of time technological opportunities vary across products and industries. As a consequence, a firm's or a nation's current specialization in production will affect its potential for future technological dynamism. Together, these insights suggest that the present allocation of resources can have a powerful effect on the direction and rate of technological advance over time.

In short, technological change is a path-dependent process in which the past affects the future scope of learning and innovation. An implication is that there may be trade-offs between an allocation of resources that is Ricardian efficient and one that yields greater technological dynamism over the long run. To understand this line of argument better, it is necessary to examine our views of the process of technological change in greater detail.

The notion of technological change which we present in this book rests on the idea that technology involves a fundamental learning aspect, often characterized by tacit and idiosyncratic knowledge and by varying degrees of cumulativeness over time. To argue this point, it is necessary to distinguish between scientific and technological knowledge, although in practice sometimes this distinction may be difficult to draw. Scientific knowledge establishes a set of basic theories, principles and premises from which technology can be built. Scientific knowledge is close to the notion of blueprint information which often characterizes discussions of technology in the traditional economics literature. Scientific knowledge can quite often be precisely specified and easily communicated in a common language. Moreover, the institutions of scientific development are international and the flow of information across national borders is extensive.

Technological knowledge, in contrast to scientific knowledge, is often local in nature in the sense that what is learned depends on the past history of technological, manufacturing and marketing successes and failures. Technological skills, competences, and organizational capabilities are all usually incrementally developed, drawing on previous strengths and experiences. As a consequence, technological knowledge is often more difficult to communicate across national borders than scientific knowledge. The transfer of a basic scientific insight from one national community of scholars to another may be quite straightforward, while the transfer of production technology may be quite difficult, as numerous case studies of technology transfer suggest.

Technological knowledge, and indeed the intellectual paradigm required to translate new technical possibilities into innovative products and processes, flows through communities as much or more than through markets. Consequently, national and sometimes even regional communities generate distinctive technological directions and trajectories. From this perspective, an important part of technological knowledge does not flow easily across national borders. Such knowledge accumulates in firms in the form of skilled workers, proprietary technology and difficult-to-copy know-how. It accumulates in communities in such diverse forms as suppliers, repair services and networks of know-how. It accumulates in nations in the skills and experiences of the workforce and in the institutions that train workers and diffuse technology. As Stowsky notes, such 'local' or non-traded knowledge is precisely the kind of knowledge that is often the most important during the initial development phase of a new product or process, knowledge that can escape the confines of a single plant or firm into regions or communities but which cannot be fully embodied in the product that is finally produced and sold. Because such knowledge is embedded in the experiences and skills of the firms and people involved in the innovation process, it does not flow easily or quickly across national borders.

Again, the processes of technological change and diffusion are rooted in existing production activities and in the linkages among sectors. Whether analysed through the optic of spillovers and externalities, the optic of linkages or other optics, the nature of linkages among sectors matter. Differences in the existing production base represent constraints and opportunities for technological development in the future.

If technological knowledge is a joint output of production so that the pace and direction of future technological change is affected by the current pattern of production, and if such knowledge is significantly local in nature, then the current pattern of a nation's production and trade specialization can have a powerful effect on its future technological trajectory. And if, as seems evident, different activities or industries differ in their technological potential, nations with different current patterns of specialization will have different long-term growth and technological prospects.

Intuitively, this seems like a strong argument for national policies to target those industries and activities with the greatest technological potential, and clearly this was an argument used by the Japanese planners. But the validity of such an argument depends on a prior demonstration of why market signals may fail to yield optimal outcomes under such circumstances. Why, in short, may there be a trade-off between patterns of resource allocation that are 'Ricardian' efficient in the short turn and those that are 'Schumpeterian' efficient in the long run? The answer to this question is found in the spillovers and imperfections inherent in the process of technological change.

Technological knowledge always involves some form of increasing returns for two reasons. First, there are usually significant set-up costs or sunk costs involved in the creation of such knowledge, as a result of which there are static economies of scale in production utilizing this knowledge. Second, there are usually significant learning effects or dynamic economies of scale in the use of such knowledge. For both reasons, the value of such knowledge is likely to increase with the scale of production.

The scope for increasing returns to technological knowledge becomes even broader once one considers the spillovers likely to exist between knowledge generated in one industry and the rest of the economy. In the presence of such spillovers, technological knowledge generated by a single activity can result in increasing returns in that activity and in other activities throughout the economy. As the history of technological change indicates, technological knowledge generated in one activity can have profound and unexpected spillover effects elsewhere. At its origin, the production of bicycles drew on technological knowledge from the production of shotguns. Innovations in food processing, even processes which do not involve any chemical inputs, draw on continuous chemical processes. Technological knowledge gained in the production of car and aeroplane manufacturing promoted innovation in machine tools and vice versa. Beer companies in Japan are currently drawing on their fermentation expertise to enter the biotechnology business. Technological complementarities, sometimes called 'untraded' interdependencies, and information flows which do not correspond to the flows of products represent a structured set of technological spillovers or externalities which form a collective asset of groups of firms or industries.

As Nathan Rosenberg, a noted economic historian of technological change, remarks: 'the ways in which technological changes coming from one industry constitute sources of technological progress and productivity growth in other industries defy easy summary or categorization ... The transmission of technological change from one sector of the economy to another ... has important implications for our understanding of the process of productivity in an economy. Specifically, a small number of industries may be responsible for generating a vastly disproportionate amount of the total technological change in an economy.'[21]

In the presence of increasing returns of spillover effects, the market cannot signal to private agents the unintended outcome of their collective behaviour. To put it differently, markets cannot deliver information about, or discount the possibility of, future states of the world whose occurrence are themselves externalities resulting from the interaction of the present decisions of behaviourally unrelated agents. Under such circumstances, there may be trade-offs between 'Ricardian' efficiency and 'Schumpeterian' efficiency. And under such circumstances policies to target activities and industries with the greatest potential for generating technological knowledge of widespread applicability throughout the economy may improve economic welfare over time. In spirit, this argument is similar to the argument of the new trade theory that policies to promote industries with technological spillovers may be welfare-improving. But the perspective here is a more dynamic one. It builds on the notion that the whole trajectory of national technological change is influenced by current patterns of resource allocation. From this perspective, the potential gains from policy intervention are not once-and-for-all but affect the entire trajectory of growth and technological progress. Such intervention, even if temporary, can have permanent effects on the future course of economic development.

SCHUMPETERIAN EFFICIENCIES AND GOVERNMENT POLICY

Investment and transformative technologies

Even if the arguments suggested here are correct, they may be questioned as a rationale for government policy. Markets at least signal present efficiencies. Future dynamic gains, precisely because they cannot be signalled and are inherently uncertain, represent a sort of policy gamble. Neither the market nor policy-makers, no matter how clever, can definitely determine whether a given industry or technological activity is a certain foundation for future growth or technological progress. Therefore, policies to target industries or activities in pursuit of growth or Schumpeterian efficiency are as likely to fail as market signals. Dynamics may matter to future economic welfare, but knowing that is not sufficient for the formulation of welfare-improving policy measures.

Our response to this line of arguments is twofold. First, we believe that at any moment of time the future social benefits of certain technologies are clearly evident. Yet because these benefits are far in excess of the privately appropriable benefits available to individual economic agents, investment in such technologies is likely to be too small to be socially optimal. We call such technologies 'strategic-transformative' technologies, because they promise radically to transform the products and production processes of a wide range of sectors that employ them and thus to have a profound effect on the competitiveness of national producers in a wide variety of world markets.[22] Today such technologies broadly include microelectronics technologies, new materials, superconductivity and biotechnologies.

Second, investments in transformative technologies can be self-fulfilling prophecies. If the initial investments are not great enough to get private producers to start up the relevant learning curves, the potential benefits of dropping prices and the extended use of such technologies in a variety of economic activities may be nil. Or, to put it differently, in the absence of policy, new technologies may not displace old ones at a socially optimal rate. The current productivity advantages of established technologies may win out over the future advantages of newer technologies, even though the former advantages may be much smaller than the latter. Determined policy efforts to pay the front end development costs or create initial markets may encourage firms to gain the knowledge to capture the benefits of the learning curve.

In recent years, Japanese targeting policies have concentrated on high-tech industries, including semiconductors, computers and telecommunications. The Japanese view these industries, like steel and shipbuilding in the past, as providing the infrastructure on which the future competitive success of a variety of sectors depends. A policy of promoting R&D and growth in these new infrastructural activities is viewed as generating beneficial effects throughout the economy. These industries provide inputs for production throughout the economy and they enjoy both static and dynamic increasing returns. Policies to promote these industries can result in lower cost inputs for a variety of user industries whose expansion in turn can feed back into still lower costs for these inputs. This virtuous interdependence between the high-tech industries and downstream users gives rise to a true externality creating process, in which private increasing returns in the high-tech industries result in social increasing returns in downstream user industries.[23]

Finally, it should be noted that the high-tech industries are strategic not only because of their linkage and knowledge externalities but also because they are characterized by imperfect competition. Take the case of new materials and biotechnology. Assume, as appears to be the case, that both technologies in a mature phase will require lower cost inputs and less energy than comparable current technologies. An energy and resource-poor nation such as Japan can reap substantial collective gains from a switch from the traditional to the new technologies. The national import will and dependence on external sources of raw materials and energy would both be reduced. Consequently, commercial advantage in specific sectors aside, there are substantial social externalities or spillovers that make it rational to use policy to promote investment in these technologies. These investments may also permit Japanese firms to have a distinct advantage in commercializing these technologies, in gaining advantage in the design of products implementing their possibilities, and in reaping a large fraction of world profits from these and related activities.

Technological trajectories, plasticity, and national settings[24]

An important lesson about the nature of technological development and the character of trajectories lies in the process by which market positions freeze after periods of fluidity. This lesson will matter as this discussion unfolds. The possibilities at the beginning of a technical transition are broad, but they narrow over time. Know-how accumulates around a particular technology. As the investment builds around the products that are succeeding in the market, alternative technical solutions become economically less attractive. Funds for experimentation in these areas dry up. Continued development therefore tends to follow lines already established.

The development of motor car engines is illustrative. One way of increasing fuel efficiency is to make cars lighter. One of the heavier components of the car is the engine. Engines could be made lighter by substituting aluminum for iron. But aluminum, though lighter, is not as durable, as strong or as easy to manipulate in the engine manufacturing processes. The technological question became whether to try to make aluminum stronger or to reduce the amount of iron in an engine to make it lighter. Iron won out in mass-production cars not because of its inherent properties but because motor engineers had much greater knowledge about it and experience with it.[25]

The direction of technological development is not determined by inherent technical characteristics or by any economic advantage that will accrue to all producers.[26] Instead, it is inherently uncertain. It depends in critical ways on chance, social conditions, corporate strategy and choice, and government policy. Take government as a case. Regulations influence the direction of private investment, and public investment shapes the economic infrastructure. Because both government policy and corporate strategy vary in different nations, the direction or technological development also differs from nation to nation. At any moment the state of science, engineering, and know-how defines a national 'technical possibility set'. But they do not define which options in the set of possibilities are exploited.

Innovations emerge from complex interaction among three factors: market demands as expressed in prices; needs that might be satisfied but are not yet expressed by buyers and sellers in the market-place, and new additions to the pool of scientific or technical knowledge. Technology is not plastic, shaped to our will. Not all things are technically possible, but technology in the long run has no internal autonomous logic that inevitably dictates its evolution or use. Technological development does not drive society as it evolves, rather technology itself is also shaped by social development. Moments of radical shifts in technology, periods of transition, are periods when political choice can exert some control over technology. Technological and social development are interactive, shaped by and shaping each other.

This line of reasoning leads us to several conclusions. If technological development is inherently uncertain, then the most conservative national or firm strategy for assuring the success of development is to spread one's bet.[27] The best analogy is to covering the table at the roulette wheel. Some might see this as a form of redundancy. We would argue that it is not. A spare tyre is redundant, but it is essential if there is a flat tyre. A second telephone line provides a cushion of capacity if the first one is in use. Both are identical to the apparatus they replace. They are quite literally redundant, or extra under ordinary conditions. Bets on a roulette wheel, however, are not identical; each is valuable precisely because it is different from the others. In terms of static efficiency, the extra or unused efforts would be duplications, wasted effort. In dynamic terms, the extra options would be duplications to guarantee success. Technology managers have often recognized this. Indeed, the Polaris submarine development programme built multiple bets into the programme at critical technological junctures.[28] The biggest technical uncertainty was whether the missiles could be fired from below the surface, and different projects were undertaken to solve the firing problem.

The multiple bets that technological development requires will not be placed evenly around the table. Instead, they will cluster in two areas, according to two principles. First, R&D bets will be historically rooted. They will reflect the past development of the firm and the national economy and tend to follow the direction of past work. The resources available for tackling the next round of technical problems will reflect what comes before. Technology has history. Second, the needs to which the technology is being applied will be different in each national community, and so the technological tasks will vary. The implications of these two principles around which technology bets cluster on the roulette table are significant.

If we accept these two principles, we are led to a range of conclusions. When a technology is in its infancy, and still fluid, the line of its technical evolution is inherently uncertain. This is not to say that all things are possible but rather that more than one direction of development is possible. An emphasis can be put on making steel stronger or lighter. The pace and direction of development are matters of decision. The direction a technology takes will depend partly on circumstance and individual choices. The directions of effort and evolution are set by the cluster of technology bets. The outcomes, the winners among competing possibilities, emerge when the sunk investment and differential learning become so great that radical alternatives are too pricy. Broad market acceptance of a new technology, for whatever reason – be it public relations or real performance – excludes new possibilities. After positions freeze, a radically new technology will not be developed unless it is so attractive that producers and users are willing to walk away from their investments in earlier technologies and, often, new entrants emerge. If the gains from new technical approaches look marginal, they will be ignored; if gains look potentially important but slow to develop or very risky, they may never be captured.

Technological development is shaped by the community in which it occurs. A trajectory of technological development is an expected outcome of a particular national community.[29] During ordinary times, when national differences produce only small branches off the main trunk of technological evolution, the ability of society to shape technology is not nearly as visible as the powerful constraints that mature technologies have set for society. Alternative routes – the roads not taken – are hidden in the past. In periods of transition, however, the direction of technology itself – its branches, not its twigs – is affected by the clustering of bets. The direction in which investment develops will be heavily influenced by where the bets are placed. That placement will depend on the needs of the national community and the resources built up during its previous development. Thus, the bet 'placer' – be it a company or a nation – actively shapes technological development. As the new branches grow, they block others from emerging.

National context, by setting the cluster of bets, shapes technology. Computer technology, for example, could grow along several different lines in the next few years. The line that wins out will reflect the historical contours and current needs of its community of origin. By blocking other options, the winning route is imposed by sustained investment on other communities. Because the winning and then dominant technological route reflects, at least in part, the historical roots and national options of a specific community, it gives at least an initial advantage to the innovating country. The technology emerges from, and plays to, the national strength of the innovating country. The winning technology always imposes its own constraints, and once set, it can shape the patterns of trade. Technology becomes a binding parameter; it does not begin as one.

We start to have the basis of a notion of technological trajectory. Learning curves and cumulative problem solving expertise, technological linkages and nationally rooted technological developments all create the basis for firms in one nation to surge to advantage in world markets together.

Market tasks, technological capacities and the emergence of new paradigms

Let us reconsider this notion of technological trajectory and national communities using a quite different kind of language. In this section we examine tasks, market and technological problems, and the capacities of firms and nations to solve them.

There is an established literature that treats the process of technological evolution at the firm level through the optic of 'search' and discovery. Different industry structures influence the 'search rules'. Differences in firm organization influence these rules. The general conjecture is that given any level of technological competence and the techniques of production which a firm can master, its specific organizational structure and strategies affect both its level of efficiency and the rates and direction of its innovation, and thus the patterns of its competitiveness over time.[30]

There is also a literature on the influence of the institutional structure of the economy on the patterns of government policy.[31] In the same fashion that an industry structure establishes a set of constraints and opportunities for firms within a sector, the options in an economy as a whole are affected by both market and institutional structures. The result is that distinctive patterns of economic response and policy characterize different nations.[32] Countries tend to respond in defined manners, in a few similar ways, to a wide range of problems. The solutions vary less than the problems. When the solution fits the problem there is a policy success, but it is hard to build a solution if the problem requires an approach outside the bounds established by the structure of the political and economic system. Consequently, nations like firms embody defined capacities. Their search for solutions is limited, like that of firms, by their structure and capacities.

Let us apply this logic to the problem of technology development and trade competition. Nations, Christopher Freeman argues, represent 'systems of innovation'. That is, they represent a set of institutions which create resources and direct them toward specific problems and solutions. When Britain opened up a major 'technological gap' in the first Industrial Revolution, this was related not simply to an increase in invention and scientific activities but to novel ways of organizing production, investment and marketing, and novel ways of combining invention with entrepreneurship. When Germany and the USA overtook Britain in the late nineteenth and twentieth centuries, their success was also related to major institutional changes in the national system of innovation, as well as to big increases in the scale of professional research and inventive activities. In particular both countries developed new ways of organizing the professional education of engineers and scientists and of organizing research and development activities as specialized departments within firms, and employing graduate engineers and scientists. Similarly today, as the opening of a new 'technology gap' by Japan and the increased 'threat' of competition from Europe and such small open economies as Canada and the Netherlands is related not simply or even mainly to the scale of R&D, but to other social and institutional changes.[33]

A national technology system represents an institutional capacity for certain tasks and distinctive weaknesses for others. A technology system, though, is not just a set of resources available for innovation and development. It is also an approach to technology and how it is used. Periodically, a cluster of new technologies and a new approach to technology, a 'techno-economic paradigm', emerges.[34] Certainly, the vast bulk of innovations are incremental or marginal changes in an existing product or process in response to market opportunities and pressures. Sometimes there are more radical innovations that are 'discontinuous events and in recent times ... usually the result of a deliberate research and development activity in enterprises and/or in university and government laboratories'.[35] Such radical innovations may serve to launch new products or so substantially improve the cost and quality of established products as new markets emerge.

More rarely, there are 'far reaching changes in technology ... [that affect] one or several sectors of the economy as well as giving rise to entirely new sectors' (ibid.). These are what we have labelled as transformative technologies. They are clusters of technologies, 'based on a combination of radical and incremental innovations together with organizational innovations' (ibid.). For example, today such clusters of innovations include synthetic materials, petrochemical innovations, injection moulding and extrusion machinery, and their applications.

Freeman argues that some changes, some clusters of innovations, are so powerful 'that they have a major influence on the behavior of the entire economy'. At issue in these cases is not simply a set of innovations, but in fact an entire way of viewing the use and application of technology.[36] The expression 'techno-economic paradigm' implies a process of economic selection from the range of the technically feasible combinations of innovations, and indeed it takes a relatively long time for a new paradigm to diffuse through the system. Such a paradigm involves a new set of 'best practice rules' and customs, new approaches to how to relate technology to market problems and new solutions to established problems. The notion of a major industrial transition, of a second industrial divide, of a shift from 'Fordist to flexible' manufacturing which has become a fad in some debates points to just such a shift in technological paradigm.[37] A radical shift in perspective opens distinctly new possibilities for productivity and competitive advantage.[38]

CONCLUSION

New paradigms change and create national development trajectories. Such new 'paradigms' do not emerge simply from a clustering of technological breakthroughs. Rather the technological breakthroughs may require a new definition and perception of a problem. Consequently, the emergence of a new technology, such as information and communications technology, does not in itself create a new paradigm. Microelectronics can be used to reinforce established mass production strategies or to implement new flexible strategies. There are certainly costs or constraints attached to the technologies themselves; they are not so flexible or plastic that they can be shaped by conception and demand to any shape and social use. The properties of specific technologies may make certain lines of development or use more difficult and others more attractive.

None the less, we postulate that the emergence of a new paradigm must be undertaken as an interplay between the community and the technical frontier. It is not by accident that nations propelling themselves into industrial prominence do so riding new sectors and new paradigms.

Section 3:

Changing access to science and technology under free trade

4 Public science, intellectual property rights and research administration

Luke Georghiou and J.S. Metcalfe

INTRODUCTION: SCIENTIFIC KNOWLEDGE AS A PUBLIC ASSET

It has long been recognized that the process of economic growth and development is dependent on the accumulation of capital. At first, economists focused attention upon the factors determining the accumulation of physical capital. But increasingly attention has shifted to less tangible forms of accumulation, specifically those which manifest themselves in the form of trained and educated human capital, and, even more generally, those that appear in the form of intellectual or knowledge capital. However, while the processes by which physical capital is accumulated and allocated are well understood, those concerned with the accumulation and allocation of intellectual or knowledge capital are less easy to comprehend and identify. As Ken Arrow has pointed out in a seminal paper,[1] the accumulation of knowledge involves indivisible investments, giving rise to increasing economies of exploitation, while there are considerable problems in establishing defensible property rights in knowledge unless the knowledge can be tied to specific artefacts. Both factors entail that the investment in new knowledge will be hindered by market imperfections and potentially improved by carefully formulated public policies. The rise to significance of the so-called 'new' or 'generic' technologies in recent years has indeed led to strong policy emphasis in many national contexts on 'strategic research'. While policy-makers have begun to accept the arguments that the results of R&D are unpredictable in both content and timing, they are no longer prepared to tolerate large-scale investment in it without some mechanism being in place to ensure that the results, when they do emerge, benefit those who made the investment in the first place. In the case of firms, the attempt is made to ensure that the resulting knowledge is proprietary, while for countries the objective is to see that exploitation of results takes place within national borders. This investment view of scientific research is central to the understanding of current policies and to the evolving network of relationships between industry and the scientific community. With an explicit focus, typical of wartime, it is increasingly argued that the technological return from investments in strategic science depends on the existence of an appropriate exploitation infrastructure. It is increasingly clear that a framework in which science institutions advance fundamental knowledge which firms acting independently then exploit is woefully inadequate. The essence of the investment view – which is becoming the dominant view within the OECD economies as trade becomes increasingly 'liberal' – is that the economic return for scientific research depends on subtle mechanisms of collaboration between the generators and the exploiters of knowledge.

In this chapter, we propose to review some of the more important issues surrounding public support of strategic science in an era of free trade. We draw attention first to two key features of strategic scientific knowledge and then proceed to a review of the emerging structures of national and international programmes to stimulate collaborative research. We then consider some of the issues which surround collaboration as a research vehicle, paying particular attention to the complex issues surrounding the identification and allocation of intellectual property rights. This leads to a discussion of cross-border restrictions on knowledge transfer. The final section considers national strategies with respect to the international division of labour in the development of strategic science.

DEFINING 'STRATEGIC' SCIENCE

It may sometimes be considered strange that technologies – such as information and communication technologies, biotechnology and new materials – should be clustered together by policy-makers and afforded similar treatment. There is much they do not have in common. Some are the basis of enormous international industries while others, such as high temperature superconductivity, are little more than promising laboratory phenomena. What they do have in common are two key features: their knowledge intensity and pervasiveness.

Knowledge intensity

Knowledge intensity is a feature of areas where intellectual capital is of high value in relation to physical capital. For example, a recent survey of major Japanese industrial companies showed that in the past few years a shift has taken place such that they now spend more on R&D then they do on capital investment.[2] In some sectors, such as pharmaceuticals, this has long been the case, but in others, such as electronics, this is a new phenomenon. As flexible manufacturing systems and other advanced manufacturing techniques take hold, it may be expected that this tendency will increase.

The implication of the importance of knowledge intensity is that a firm's ability to enhance its own knowledge base is a key aspect of competitive performance. As Itami[3] has argued, competitive advantage depends on the accumulation of invisible assets. The crucial point here is that the relevant knowledge base is structured. Since the knowledge base of the firm is part of a wider knowledge base with which it needs to communicate, it is important to address the question of structure. Figure 4.1 illustrates two dimensions of the knowledge base. On the vertical axis of the matrix the distinction is made between public and proprietary knowledge. The horizontal axis uses Polanyi's categories of codified and tacit knowledge.[4] Thus, we have knowledge that is codifiable and public (such is found in scientific or

	Codified	Tacit
Public	e.g. Publications	Generic e.g. Skills
Proprietary	e.g. Patents	Firm-specific skills e.g. Know-how

Figure 4.1 The Manchester Matrix

technical publications). The output of public domain work may well include the frequent acquisition or imparting of generic skills through public training and education programmes, and hence may be tacit rather than codified. Moving to proprietary knowledge, this too may be codified in the form of internal company documents of patents, and again there exists a corresponding body of tacit knowledge in the form of specific skills which, this time, is exclusive to the firm. Corresponding to the different sectors of the matrix are different knowledge-generating institutions and different mechanisms for the accumulation of knowledge. Universities and public research laboratories demonstrate the public-codified segment and accumulate knowledge in a relatively open and unstructured fashion. They are driven by the internal dynamics of the scientific community. Private companies generate codified and tacit knowledge through focused R&D programmes and through various learning mechanisms which are inseparable from the production and marketing activities of the firm. The boundaries between the sectors of the matrix are, to different degrees, permeable and much recent policy concern is concerned with this permeability issue under the general guise of technology transfer.

With this simple framework, it is possible to begin to explore the structure of knowledge bases. To return to generic technologies, it is characteristic of them that a substantial part of the knowledge base lies in the public sector. In part, this is due both to the novelty of the technologies themselves *and* to their rate of development. The latter feature creates an environment of uncertainty for companies and hence imports a greater incentive to keep in touch with alternative options to those which the company is backing. Most significantly, the distribution of the knowledge base makes it essential for companies in these areas to have the capacity to monitor and absorb knowledge from public sector science institutions, notably universities.

To meet this need, a variety of mechanisms has been – and will continue to be –developed to facilitate this technology transfer and to supplement the traditional method of transferring tacit knowledge via the recruitment of students. Such mechanisms concentrate on academic-industrial collaboration and are discussed in detail later. For the time being, the point to note is that to exploit the knowledge thus transferred, firms need to establish proprietary rights. The issue of these intellectual property rights forms the main theme of this chapter. We shall argue that the protection necessary for successful industrial exploitation can affect the university research enterprise itself and its mechanisms of knowledge accumulation through the traditional free flow of knowledge upon which it is based.

Knowledge flows are not, of course, exclusively between the cells of the matrix. They are also extensive within them. Even in the proprietary domain, work by Von Hippel[5] and others has shown that know-how flows between firms through informal professional networks as well as by the transfer of personnel. Inter-firm collaboration is another emergent phenomenon which results in transfer of knowledge between firms, both deliberately (within the scope of collaboration) and unintentionally, through the increase in contact this brings about.

Pervasiveness

Before considering the phenomenon of collaborative research, it is worth discussing the implications of the other characteristics of the generic technologies – their pervasiveness. This feature, the fact that they have application in a wide range of productive activities, largely explains the prominence afforded them by policy-makers. Their priority is also founded upon expectations of the industrial activity they may generate directly – as Patel and Pavitt argue in Chapter 5 – although not every country can reasonably expect to succeed in the same technologies as its competitors. The fundamental point is that pervasiveness can have a large impact in restructuring patterns of international comparative advance such as we are likely to see under 'Europe 1992'. Pervasiveness itself shows up in at least two manifestations:

(*i*) where the technology underpins a narrow range of products which themselves have a wide range of applications; and

(*ii*) where the technology directly supports a wide range of products.

An example of the first case would be microchips and of the second a biotechnology-based technique such as protein engineering. The second type of manifestation is inherently more amenable to the appropriation of technology through its embodiment in products or processes. As a result, intellectual property rights are more significant in such types. In the first case, other barriers exist, such as the need for large-scale capital investment to achieve economies of scale. In the second case, investments and critical masses are likely to be much smaller. The implication of the characteristics of pervasiveness is that it is unrealistic to discuss the rules for accumulating knowledge without also considering the rules for its subsequent exploitation.

Given their features of knowledge intensity and pervasiveness, it follows that the generic technologies have significant implications for competitive activity and that the development of a technology base is expansive. Both elements combine to encourage collaboration as a route to knowledge acquisition. The central points here can be illustrated with respect to the concept of the time–cost trade-off in the development of a competitive technological capability (see Figure 4.2.) Curve a–a shows the relationship between the cost of knowledge generation and the time taken to generate a specified level of performance in a particular technology. The higher the level of required performance the further to the right lies this time–cost trade-off. On the trade-off curve, if the level of effort drops below 0_x, the capability which will never be acquired to this level corresponds to the minimum threshold of effort.

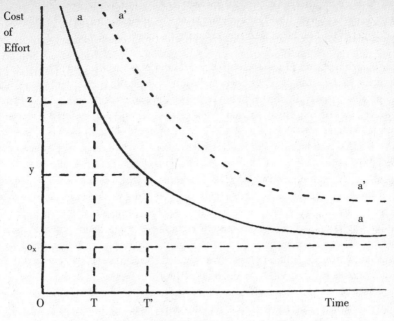

Figure 4.2 The time–cost trade-off

Now suppose that firms in a competing nation make a credible announcement to the effect that they will introduce the technology to a given level of specification at time T. Imagine that this creates the competitive window $T-T^1$, entry after T^1 not yielding any commercial advantage. Then this country must make a cumulative investment of at least O_z if it is to gain any competitive advantage, and at least O_y if it is to introduce the technology at the same time as its international rivals. The case for collaboration arises directly when the scale of effort which can be mounted by national firms and knowledge institutions operating individually is less than O_z so that the window of competitive opportunity is missed. Without collaboration, the individual firm is left with the only possibility of introducing the technology at the same time as its international rivals. By collaborating, parallel strands of investigation can be pursued while duplication of effort can be avoided, risks spread, and the cumulative value of effort brought within the required range.[6] Such is the basic case for collaborating in the development of generic technologies. Later we will delve more deeply into the qualifications which need to surround the time-cost trade-off, but for the moment we consider some recent cases of collaboration.

INTERNATIONAL AND NATIONAL STIMULATION OF COLLABORATIVE RESEARCH

Models of academic–industrial collaboration

As noted above, the rise of the generic technologies has coincided with the emergence of a variety of models for academic–industrial collaboration. These models are distinguished in several dimensions including degree of contact, the degree of control over the research performed and the treatment of intellectual property generated under their terms. Some of the main forms are:

(*i*) *Bilateral contracts* In countries where universities are allowed to perform work for industry these arrangements most commonly involve the performance of research in a specified area with the company holding all exploitation rights in return for providing cash or facilities. An emergent phenomenon, particularly favoured by Japanese companies overseas, is the establishment of campus-based research centres designed to tap into the leading centres of knowledge. A recent example is the establishment of four Hitachi research centres in the USA and Europe. At Cambridge University in England, the company will contribute a substantial proportion of the cost of a new microelectronics building in return for use of some of the space and the right to establish joint research projects in return for further funding. The company will retain patent rights to these projects but will pay the university about 50 per cent of patent royalties. These arrangements may be distinguished from consultancy-type arrangements (undertaken by some institutions or individuals motivated solely by the financial return) by the relative freedom given to researchers to pursue their scientific interests. Presumably the companies involved recognize that they cannot second guess leading researchers and simply wish to have a presence if exploitable results emerge. Geographical proximity to the company's manufacturing operation does not appear to be necessary. In the case of Japanese companies in Europe, the research centres rarely relate to their European manufacturing interests.

(*ii*) *Priority programmes* Since the late 1970s, research councils in most countries have diversified from their traditional responsive modes to national interest. An early example of this was the foundation by the (then) UK Science Research Council of its first two directorates, in Polymer Engineering and Marine Technology. These aimed to attract researchers into areas of industrial priority and operated largely through modification of the project selection process to include priority areas, industrial members of peer-review panels and a programme director with limited delegated powers to award grants. Although industrial relevance was a strongly emphasized criterion, industry did not necessarily have to participate in the research or have privileged access to results. Nevertheless, as time passed, the Marine Technology Directorate gradually increased the level of the criterion of industrial relevance from expressions of support to the point where industry was expected to contribute matching funds to managed programmes of academic research. These directorates have now been 'privatized' (i.e. are no longer part of the Science and Engineering Research Council) with the function of acting as brokers for academic–industrial collaboration. Van Rossum[7] has reviewed Research Council responses to initiatives of this kind in Sweden, Switzerland and the Federal Republic of Germany, and has noted the emergence of role conflicts as a result.

(*iii*) *Research centres* Directed programmes act upon the existing system and do not attempt to alter research structures. This may lead to a problem in that university departmental delineations reflect primarily the teaching needs of the institution and are generally strongly aligned to traditional disciplinary boundaries. Research problems, particularly those of an industrial kind, tend to be interdisciplinary and may not map well onto these existing structures. To some extent networking between locations may address this but a more radical response has been to concentrate researchers in interdisciplinary research centres. An early example of this was the US National Science Foundation's University–Industry Co-operative Research Centres, now superseded by the Engineering Research Centres. It is an explicit part of the rationale of the latter that they develop knowledge in areas that will help US industry improve its industrial competitiveness for markets at home and abroad over the long term.

The research centre concept has extended beyond the purely academic domain to include industrial and government researchers. Here the model has come from Japan where the perceived success of the Very Lareg Scale Integration (VLSI) project in the late 1970s formed the role model for pre-competitive research programmes in Europe and the USA. Under this model, companies share the costs and risks of performing R&D, in this case in a common location, and then each use the results independently to compete in the market. This is a somewhat idealized structure since, even in Japan, companies dislike working with their true competitors and in that case most of the key work was performed by larger teams working within the companies' own research divisions. In Western industrialized countries, centres such as the Micro-electronics and Computer Technology Corporation (MCC) in the USA have faced difficulties in persuading participating companies to second staff because, unlike Japan, such staff have high mobility and may not return. Furthermore, for the individuals concerned, a long-term secondment may be perceived as impeding career prospects. The response has been to hire researchers on the open market directly for the centre. The problem then becomes one of technology transfer – the difficulty of conveying results back to the sponsor companies. The research itself is also in danger of becoming remote from the commercial concerns of the companies.

As academic centres of excellence proliferate, similar issues may be expected to materialize. New centres may have difficulty attracting top quality staff, while those built upon existing institutions or departments may not affect the desired cultural shift. In this case, unlike that of the industrial centres, the structure is intended to be more amenable to transfer of knowledge than that which it replaces, but other than addressing a problem couched in interdisciplinary terms, there seems no reason why simply the fact of having a centre will facilitate transfer.

(*iv*) *Academic–industrial programmes* In contrast to the research council programmes discussed above, in which academic research is channelled into priority areas and industrial contact and contributions are fostered, the 1980s have seen a new model of collaboration emerge. In this model, programmes aimed primarily at industrial objectives seek to involve academic researchers working jointly with teams from participating firms. An early example of this was the United Kingdom's Alvey Programme for Advanced Information Technology, followed closely by the European Commission's ESPRIT 1 Programme which addressed similar technological areas on a European scale. In each case the bulk of the funding went to firms to perform R&D, generally on their own premises, in collaboration with other firms. However, the collaborative projects also frequently involved academic teams, sometimes large ones. The sheer scale of these programmes meant that the academic component, though small in proportion to industry's share, was very large by the normal standards of university research funding. Evaluations of these programmes have indicated that, though the universities brought in valuable expertise, their role was not unusually critical to the project. Typically they were exploring longer term options with the effect of raising the technology level of the project.

Outside the area of information technology there has been less emphasis on major programmes of industrial support. Programmes in biotechnology, for example, have stressed scientific rather than industrial goals. This is illustrated by the European Commission's first two biotechnology actions: the Biomolecular Engineering Programme and the Biotechnology Action Programme. Here, a recent evaluation[8] found that few firms participated in the programmes. One reason suggested was that, in biotechnology, even quite basic research may lead to patentable – and therefore commercially valuable – inventions, thus lending weight to the distinction in types of pervasiveness already made. The difference in type of support programme in part lies in the relative maturity of the fields and the structure of the knowledge base. Another related dimension is the lobbying power of the relevant industry, and here information technology, with its long-standing relations with governments through defence and telecommunications procurement, holds an advantage.

A new basis for collaboration

If the gamut of models of academic–industrial collaboration is considered, it emerges that a new basis now exists for interaction. Traditionally there was a linear model in which academics did science and industry exploited it. The two activities were kept in separate conceptual boxes. Policy debates considered whether the output of academic research or the way in which it was performed was amenable to exploitation. The evolution of the mechanisms for supporting academic–industrial collaboration has been a shift from broad priority setting in terms of industrial goals, through a period where demonstrable industrial interest was a requirement, to the current situation where *active* collaboration is sought. Technology transfer is no longer an adjunct or sequential follow-on to research, it is now built into the structure of the work itself. In many ways, this development is to be welcomed since the type of knowledge-enhancing work often performed by universities is not easily codifiable in a form that industry can absorb. In a fully collaborative project the frequent contacts, seminars, interchange of personnel and sharing of common goals create an environment where the barriers of the NIH ('Not Invented Here') syndrome may be lowered.

Realization of the benefits afforded by collaboration of this kind is, however, difficult. The greatest barrier to be overcome is cultural. It might be expected that academics hitherto used to a responsive peer-review based funding system would be resistant to the idea of directed research, but this has not generally been the case. To some extent the consultation carried out prior to the formulation of workplans and strategies has built into them the demands of the community. True difficulties are more evident at the implementation phase. A frequent finding from evaluations is that industrial participants find their academic partners 'hard to manage'. This results from the failure of academic researchers to meet the deadlines and reporting requirements common in industrial research. Doubtless, there are cases of individual laxity but much of this cultural gap is rooted in the difference in the nature of research performed (academic research is more open-ended and often appears to lack internal structure). While such an approach may work well for individual researchers or small teams, the effect of the funding levels of some of these projects has been to provide universities with very large teams and consequently a new order of management demands.

The structural changes imposed upon academic research by the demands of collaboration have coincided with a period when the same institutions have been ever more actively seeking alternative funding sources to their traditional base. Though generous funding has been available for the generic technological areas, this has not been the case for some institutional funding which has ceased to grow or has declined in real terms. The search to develop alternative income sources has included the kind of bilateral arrangements described in the previous section on academic–industrial collaboration, but has also encompassed efforts to exploit directly the intellectual property rights (IPR) generated through research performed in the institution either by licensing or even by manufacturing in a subsidiary company. The question of IPR is discussed below, but a point which may be made here is that pursuance of income in this way changes the basis of the relationship with industry since now *both* parties are seeking to appropriate the relevant knowledge and hence a level of competition is introduced into their relationship.

Intellectual property rights

The generation and allocation of intellectual property is a key to the incentive structures which shape the development of science and technology. In science, intellectual property is identified and allocated through priority in publication: in technology it is identified and allocated through a combination of the patent system and secrecy. Quite clearly the cultures within science differ fundamentally from those within technology and this has considerable significance for the development of strategic science.

Just as the forms and structures of academic–industrial collaboration vary, so do the IPR arrangements which underpin them. Before discussing the details of these, it is worth noting that IPR arrangements govern future use of research results not only in the context of exploitation but also in the context of follow-on research. In addition, they cover the use of 'background', that is the previous knowledge brought to the project by participants. The approach of different programmes towards ownership of results has differed markedly. In the United Kingdom two conflicting trends have coincided. On the one hand, in an attempt to encourage exploitation, a new regime was introduced from 1984 governing the ownership of research funded by research councils. Previously, rights to exploitation had been vested in the British Technology Group (formerly the National Research and Development Corporation), a state-owned body which licensed technology to industry. Under the new regime, rights reverted to academic institutions, with special provision also made for individual inventors.

Universities were not able to benefit from the changes in respect of collaborative research programmes, however, because here all property rights were vested in their industrial partners. These were codified in the framework document for the

Alvey programme and repeated in subsequent initiatives, notably the LINK model which is now used in the United Kingdom across a wide range of science and technology areas. In return for loss of ownership of results, academic participants were to receive royalties on their contributions to any eventual products, and rights to use their contributions to any eventual products, and they would receive payment for use of any 'background' IPR they brought into the projects.

The net effect of these changes was to create a situation of confusion in which some projects suffered protracted delays while arguments proceeded over the detailed terms of the collaboration agreements which embodied these arrangements. The irony of the situation is that, in retrospect, it is now clear that the type of pre-competitive research undertaken in this type of programme rarely produces the sort of results which are amenable to calculation of royalties. Even where they are, attributing the contribution of an academic partner to a product is very difficult, given the number of intervening factors prior to successful innovation (e.g. development, investment and marketing). More often, the resulting knowledge is of a tacit nature and is exploited by improving the technology level of the industrial partner across a wide range of products and processes.

In any event, royalties are not a major motivation for academic participants. The European Community's ESPRIT programme treats all participants equally and therefore academic participants do receive IPR. However, since participants have free use of their partners' results, no royalties are involved. Sub-licensing of results may be prohibited if this threatens a participant's 'major business interests' and so universities may be required to exploit directly and this rarely happens. The inference is that academics remain primarily motivated by funding for their research. Their most lucrative route to economic return lies in direct marketing of their expertise on a consultancy basis.

An emergent problem is that as the first generation of collaborative programmes comes to an end it creates a body of knowledge owned jointly by the partners in each project. In the second generation of these programmes, new groupings are emerging which mix ownership of the results of the preceding projects. Since these results are often a necessary precondition for future research, complex patterns of ownership and interdependency are emerging which may inhibit exploitation of the results of the current programmes. On the other hand, firms and universities which have been through the experience of first generation collaboration appear to have acquired skills in the management of all aspects of this activity, including IPR arrangements, which make them better able to handle problems of this nature.

The impact of collaboration

At the outset we suggested that the demand for the protection of knowledge that is necessary for successful exploitation could affect the university research enterprise itself. This is not the only effect. Several influences, sometimes countervailing each other, have an impact. The first set of issues concerns the impact upon the scale of research. By and large, the effect of industrial collaboration on university research is to increase the amount of funding available for research. Some of the funds, though, may be diverted from responsive funding and, given the scarcity of good quality researchers, there is an opportunity cost to basic research. The cost of collaboration in terms of time and effort also can reduce the time available for research.

The second set of issues concerns the agenda for research. All models of collaboration involve some direction being imposed upon the academic researchers. This direction may be indicative (identifying general areas for which funding is available) or specific – some programmes invite bids for specific projects. In those cases where the academic researchers are obliged to collaborate with industrial partners, the resulting project will represent a compromise of their interests. Hence academic researchers either have to modify their interests or else see funding going to those who work in the selected areas.

Neither of the two above effects should be regarded as deleterious. If science uses the investment argument as a basis for obtaining funding, then it is not unreasonable that the investors should seek to direct the research into areas where they have the capacity to exploit results. However, where the research enterprise is likely to suffer is in the situation where restrictions on publication or other forms of dissemination of results slow down the ability to absorb and build on the work of others. So far, this appears not to have been a major problem but potentially it could become so. Scientists may end up having to choose which reward system they prefer to operate under.

CROSS-BORDER RESTRICTIONS ON KNOWLEDGE TRANSFER

The traditional norms of the scientific community have recognized no frontiers, with published science belonging to that community as a whole. Even as sociologists such as R.K. Merton were writing of the scientific 'ethos'[9] they were noting the inherent conflicts which science has with the state. Today the pressures on science to conform to externally derived rules are far greater. One dimension of this problem resides in defence concerns, that rapid advances in information technology in particular have conferred a strategic advantage upon the Western alliance which justifies extraordinary measures to maintain it. This mode of thought was given a further boost by the Star Wars programme. Authors such as MacDonald *et al.* have covered the implications of export controls and these will not be addressed further here.

There remains a second dimension within which the pressure upon science to deviate from its norms derives from concern for national industrial competitiveness. In the USA and Europe restrictions are beginning to emerge – quite independent of trade liberalization – upon the cross-border transfer of scientific knowledge. The best-known example perhaps was the exclusion of non-US nationals from early meetings regarding high temperature superconductivity. In Europe the arguments have concerned the rights of foreign-owned multinationals to participate in government-sponsored programmes. Some countries, particularly those without a well-developed industrial base, are concerned that their participation in programmes such as ESPRIT is largely confined to university-based teams. They fear that the programmes will result in countries that are already behind functioning as net exporters of knowledge.

It seems unavoidable that restrictions of this kind would appear. Two basic reasons underpin this emergence:

the justification of science funding on a competitiveness rationale; and

the perception of substantial imbalances in cross-border knowledge flows.

The first reason relates to the arguments set out earlier in this chapter, that investment in generic technologies is justified in terms of their strategic value. Although, as remarked above, the exploitation route is neither direct nor obvious, the strong stress by the scientific establishment on the investment value of supporting research in these areas creates a climate in which returns are expected. Since the investors are national governments acting on behalf of national industry, the temptation is to try to ensure that the benefit accrues where it is intended.

This would be less of a problem if knowledge generated in the nation's public sector institutions was not easily appropriable by foreign firms. In practice though, the experience has been that some countries, notably Japan, have benefited from the second factor, imbalances in knowledge flows. This is a situation which has resulted in the Japanese government launching programmes such as the Human Frontiers Initiatives not only to strengthen its own knowledge base but also to be seen as a contributor to international knowledge flows and hence not be excluded from access to ideas generated elsewhere.

The true extent to which knowledge flow is artificially restricted must be in doubt, whatever the intentions of policy-makers, simply because the international mobility of scientists is relatively high. Although the codified knowledge may be proprietary and therefore subject to restriction, the tacit store of knowledge may be tapped by enlisting the former project personnel to work in a related area. In terms of scope, programmes with the type of IPR regimes which restrict scientific interchange are still perhaps at the margins of science, but these margins are the growth points, and are often in the most exciting areas.

There remains the issue of whether cross-border restrictions are likely to penetrate to other areas of science within the 'core'. This seems unlikely since both commercial pressures and the available levers are less here. However, a more natural barrier should not be forgotten. This is that technology transfer between research and industry is itself so difficult that appropriating knowledge from a distance becomes a formidable task.

DIVISION OF LABOUR

Up to this point we have dwelt upon the concerns which exist about knowledge flows. However, the vast and fast-moving body of knowledge which underpins the development of the generic technologies is beyond the capabilities of most nations (with the possible exceptions of the USA and Japan) to cover comprehensively. If a nation can afford only partial coverage and is not to spread its resources too thinly, then two options appear to be available, either:

(i) select priority areas in the light of national interests and capabilities and downgrade funding in other areas; or

(ii) broaden coverage by means of an explicit strategy of international collaboration.

Significant constraints exist on both of these. Past attempts to pick winners have been fraught with errors and a country runs the risk of abandoning some future vital areas. The fundamental issue here is the extent to which the science which is dropped is available as an international public good. It is simply not the case that scientific knowledge is available without cost to those nations not participating in its generation. Moreover, as we have seen, the chances are diminishing that other nations will tolerate free riding behaviour in the exploitation of science.

In Figure 4.2 we introduced the concept of a research time–cost trade-off and the related concept of an effort threshold, that minimum investment required to have any strategic competence in a particular scientific area. In effect, the threshold level of effort constitutes a watching brief from which a country may develop a more comprehensive programme should it wish. As yet we know very little about the determinants of watching brief levels of effort. No doubt they are greater the more rapid the general pace of advance in a given field is and the more capital intensive the experimental technology is. At the same time, the more narrow the focus of the watching brief, the more difficult it will be to break out into related areas essential for the strategic development of the science. Fundamental here is the point that exploitation is inherently interdisciplinary and that it is extremely difficult to forecast the precise web of needed disciplines in advance. One missing link can jeopardize a country's entire exploitation capability. Clearly these considerations add to the dangers of a 'too-narrow watching brief' approach.

It is no doubt partially to avoid those difficulties that in recent years we have seen the emergence of collaborative international research programmes. In these, countries attempt to take account of the international division of labour in scientific effort while maintaining open access to a wide spectrum of scientific output. In this way they can exploit the constraints of the time–cost trade-off and ensure that no single partner gains a significant lead time in access to key results. However, it must be recognized here that equality in terms of access to research results does not imply equality in the ability to exploit those results.

While collaborative programmes bring the benefits of pooled resources and enable a country to shift its position on the time–cost trade-off, it must also be recognized that international collaboration may entail adverse shifts in the relation between effort and results. As shown in Figure 4.2, the difficulties of collaborating may shift the trade-off upwards (dotted curve). The principal difficulties which can be identified arise from the establishment of new administrative structures in which all the participants suffer from liabilities of newness. Formal and informal patterns of behaviour have to be learnt and agreement has to be reached on both strategic objectives and their mode of implementation. This is one reason why those who have collaborated previously are reluctant to admit new inexperienced partners into collaborative arrangements. Making collaborations effective requires a substantial indivisible investment on the part of the participating nations and institutions. Thus, with the accumulation of collaborative experience, adverse shifts in the time–cost trade-off can be minimized.

CONCLUSION

In this chapter, we have explored some of the issues which surround the production of knowledge as a strategic national asset. The internationalization of markets in commodities and capital, a strong feature of the third quarter of this century, has been followed by increasing internationalization of the 'market' for strategic scientific knowledge. But markets in knowledge are inherently imperfect and nowhere are these imperfections clearer than with respect to the problems of IPR and collaboration in strategic scientific endeavour. The open community of science finds that it must integrate more closely with companies which are dependent upon establishing proprietary rights if they are to exploit knowledge in more open trading regimes to their competitive advantage. At root we have a clash between quite different cultures heightened by the structure of the knowledge bases appropriate to the new technologies as reflected in pervasiveness and intensity. To cope with this clash, new varieties of procedures for administering and exploiting research have been developed, procedures which emphasize close integration between the exploiters of research and its generators such that the knowledge production and exploitation phases are indistinguishable. It is for this reason that knowledge generated in this fashion is aptly termed 'strategic'.

5 The nature, determinants, and implications of uneven technological development

Pari Patel and Keith Pavitt

INTRODUCTION

Technological activities are a major determinant of economic performance in industrialized market economies, and, given the current political interests in moving towards more liberalized trade and larger trading blocks, technologies will only become more important for firms and nations. Indeed this prediction can be supported by the observation that international differences in productivity and trade performance can be explained at the firm, sector and national level in terms of technological gaps, and more precisely in terms of international differences in the volume or intensity of technological activities.[1] Thus, as future markets are re-shaped and competition is expanded, better understanding of the nature and determinants of technological activities will become increasingly important for both theory and policy.

In order to move towards such an understanding, the essential – if stark – distinction that we eventually make in this chapter is between national economic systems that are technologically dynamic and those that are technologically myopic. For our purposes, the former recognizes the cumulative, irreversible and uncertain nature of technological activities, whereas the latter does not. In myopic systems, technological activities are evaluated like an ordinary investment, namely, on the basis of their prospective rate of return in responding to an existing and precise market demand, and with heavy discounts for time and risk. In dynamic systems, on the other hand, the evaluation of technological activities also includes the prospect of creating and capturing new markets, and of accumulating – over time – the knowledge and experiences that open up further technological applications and business opportunities in the future.

On this basis, what would we expect to be the key measurable differences between technologically dynamic and myopic systems? This is a question which we try to answer, in part, in the pages that follow. In general we shall suggest that dynamic systems have greater access to long-term financing, relatively more scientists and engineers in management, a more highly trained workforce, and greater intra-firm flexibility towards emerging technological opportunities.

Within this dynamic/myopic framework, this chapter uses a variety of measures to compare the level and composition of technological activities in Western Europe, the USA and Japan. These measures reveal several consistent patterns, the most noteable of which are:

(*i*) marked differences in technological activity within Western Europe: high levels in West Germany, Sweden and Switzerland; relatively low levels and weak trends in the UK and the Netherlands; and strong upward trends in Belgium, France and Italy;

(*ii*) a weakening of aggregate performance of US firms, coupled with growing specialization in defence and natural resource-based technologies; and

(*iii*) a high level and strong upward trend in aggregate technological activity in Japan, with particular strength in electronics and automobiles.

In order to trace these technological activities, we shall begin by discussing the nature of technology and technological change, questions relating to firm size, sectoral patterns of technological accumulation and inter-sectoral variations. We shall conclude with some remarks on dynamic and myopic system, and their implications for freer trade.

THE NATURE OF TECHNOLOGICAL ACTIVITIES

The nature of technology

We define technology as knowledge that contributes to the creation, production and improvement of economically and socially useful products and services. Such knowledge thus relates not only to physical artefacts but also to forms of organization for their production, distribution and use. Our analysis will concentrate on knowledge related to physical artefacts rather than to organization, since it is easier to measure, and since it develops in ways that are parallel and complementary to organizational knowledge.

We depart clearly from the widely held assumption that technology is a form of 'information', that has the properties of being costly to produce, but virtually costless to transfer and to use (and by implication, widely applicable in the first place). On the contrary, technological knowledge is often tacit (i.e. cannot be made fully explicit in the form of instructions or codes of operation) and mostly specific to firms and to particular classes of product and production process. This knowledge is generated in large part not through 'research' activities but through full-time or part-time innovative activities undertaken in firms to develop and improve specific products and production processes.[2] Depending on the type of technology, industry, firm or innovation, such activities might be defined mainly as 'Design', 'Development' or 'Production Engineering'. And with the increasing efficiency and diffusion of information technology, software is becoming an increasingly important locus of technology, emerging mainly from 'systems groups' and 'systems houses'.

Both technology acquisition and related innovative activities are essentially cumulative processes. Given the firm-specific and differentiated nature of products, processes and related technological knowledge, firms do not engage in comprehensive and complete research activities but explore technological and market zones contiguous to their existing activities: what firms try to do technologically in the future is strongly conditioned by what they have been able to do in the past.

Sources of technological change

Given these characteristics, we reject the two extreme models of the innovation process and technological change. The first can be described as the 'science push' or 'linear' model, where 'R' leads to 'D', then to 'innovation' (i.e. first commercialization) and then to 'diffusion' amongst the potential population of users. It is sometimes assumed in such models that 'inventions' – as measured through patenting – are an intermediate 'output' of R&D activities, and that the nature of an innovation and of related technology remains the same throughout the process of diffusion. The second model can be described as 'demand pull', and assumes that the rate and direction of technological change are by-products of other forms of economic activity: in particular, investment in plant and equipment is assumed to be both the means through which inventions are commercialized, as well as the mechanism for inducing innovative activities upstream in related capital goods.

Whilst both these models do reflect observable dimensions of technological change, they have a number of limitations. First, they ignore the importance in innovative activities of interaction and balance between 'science push' and 'demand pull'. They also ignore the very considerable variation amongst sectors, products and technologies. Thus, whilst scientific research has enabled radical innovations in chemicals and electronics, its major function in most other industries is to help provide trained technological personnel, and to be one of the sources of background information for technological problem-solvers.[3] Similarly, whilst investment activity is the driving force behind the inducement and commercialization of innovations in steel-making and many other process industries, it is almost entirely a derived function of success in product innovation (with a strong element of 'science push') in sectors like pharmaceuticals.[4]

These characteristics of technology and its determinants have a number of implications. They help to explain the considerable variation amongst firms, in the same national and international market environment, in the level and composition of their innovative activities. In part, these reflect the well-known and considerable *ex ante* uncertainties surrounding innovative activities. They also reflect what Atkinson and Stiglitz pointed out some time ago:[5] when technology is localized in firms and cumulative in development, decisions about investments in technology reflect both past patterns of innovative activity, and expectations about the future, both of which are firm-specific. Furthermore, given that technological change is firm-specific and cumulative, the sectoral technological strengths and weaknesses of firms and countries do not change rapidly over time. This means that their technological patterns and trends in the recent past are a reliable guide to events in the not too distant future.[6] It also means that our statistical comparisons can be seen as an attempt to measure and compare levels and composition of 'technological accumulation' or 'technological capital' across regions and countries.

Second, the process of technological accumulation is not synonymous with the processes of either physical capital accumulation or scientific progress, even if it overlaps with both of them. We concentrate our analysis here on innovative activities and technology. Here, the clear distinctions in the 'linear' model amongst invention, innovation and diffusion do not reflect the more complex and interactive reality: 'invention' is often induced in order to solve problems of innovation, whilst diffusion almost always involves further technology and innovation, if only to adapt the innovation to the specific skill, factor and product markets of adopting firms. Measured aspects of innovative activities – such as R&D or patenting – are undertaken in relation to the invention, commercialization, diffusion and adaptation of innovations.

Technological activities in firms

Technological activities are undertaken by firms with the intention of either getting ahead of, or keeping up with, their competitors. The creation of firm-specific technological knowledge involves the design, development and testing of products and production processes, followed by learning by doing (for processes), by using and by failing (for products), and comprising much tacit (i.e. uncodifiable) knowledge. Scientific theory is rarely sufficiently robust to predict the performance of a technological artefact under operating conditions with a high enough degree of certainty to eliminate the costly and time-consuming construction and testing of prototypes and pilot plant. Since technology is largely firm-specific, in-house technological competence is essential for the exploitation of scientific and technological opportunities; lags in catching up with frontier technology often result from the lack of such competence rather than from legal, informational, policy or other types of barriers to entry.[7]

The rate and direction of firms' technological activities are a function of their size and principal business. Thus, innovating small firms are typically specialized in their technological strategies, concentrating on product innovation in specific producer goods, such as machine tools, scientific instruments, specialized chemicals or software. Their key strategic strengths are in the ability to match technology with specific customer requirements. The key strategic tasks are finding and maintaining a stable product niche, and benefiting systematically from user experience. Large innovating firms, on the other hand, are typically broad front in their technological activities, and divisionalized in their organization. The key technological strengths can be based on R&D laboratories (typically in chemicals and electrical-electronic products), or in the design and operation of complex production technology (typically in mass production and continuous process industries), and – increasingly – in complex information processing technology (typically in finance and retailing).[8]

INTERNATIONAL COMPARISONS OF TECHNOLOGICAL ACTIVITIES

Statistics on the international distribution of the sources of US patenting show highly significant similarities to those on business enterprise R&D expenditures, both in aggregate and in specific sectors.[9] In Tables 5.1 to 5.3 below, we summarize the main features of the international distribution of technological activities, as reflected in available data on R&D activities and on US patenting. Tables 5.1 and 5.2 compare the proportions of national resources devoted to technological activities. Table 5.1 uses the proportion of industrial output spent on industrial R&D. It distinguishes between 'Total' and 'Industry-financed' R&D, the difference between the two being mainly government-funded defence R&D, performed in the aerospace and electronics sectors. The UK and USA compare more favourably with other countries in total industrial R&D, reflecting their relatively large commitment to defence R&D. Table 5.2 compares the number of US patents per capita, which shows international patterns and trends very similar to those in industry-financed R&D as a proportion of industrial output. Table 5.3 uses the US patenting statistics, broken down into nine broad sectors of technology, to identify countries' sectoral strengths and weaknesses, as measured by their patterns of 'Revealed Technology Advantage' (RTA) – defined as the ratios of each country's share of US patenting in the sectors, to its share of total US patenting. As such it is similar to the concept of

Table 5.1 Trends in industrial R&D as a proportion of industrial output in some OECD countries: 1967–85

	Total			Industry-Financed[a]		
	1967	*1975*	*1985*	*1967*	*1975*	*1985*
Japan	0.92	1.28	2.11	0.90	1.26	2.07
United States of America	2.35	1.84	2.32	1.15	1.18	1.54
France	1.36	1.36	1.78	0.75	0.87	1.24
Federal Republic of Germany	1.31	1.65	2.42	1.07	1.30	1.99
Italy	0.43	0.61	0.92	0.41	0.55	0.71
Netherlands	1.45	1.45	1.50	1.31	1.30	1.22
Sweden	1.29	1.64	3.03	0.94	1.48	2.64
Switzerland	n.a.	n.a.	n.a.	n.a.	n.a.	n.a.
United Kingdon	2.01	1.72	2.01	1.34	1.08	1.32
Western Europe[b]	1.27	1.35	1.81	0.92	1.00	1.37

a Industry-financed R&D excludes that funded by government.
b West Europe is defined as the seven European countries listed above plus Belgium, Denmark, and Ireland. The total R&D and industrial output for Europe have been calculated by first transforming each country's data into US dollars on the basis of purchasing power parities and then aggregating.

Source: OECD.

'revealed comparative advantage', defined as the ratio of a country's share of world exports in a sector to its share of total world exports, and used to measure countries' sectors of relative trading strength. In both cases, a ratio greater than unity reflects relative strength, and less than unity relative weakness. These tables are the basis of the descriptions of countries' technological activities that we present below. We also draw on analyses of the origins of highly cited US patents, and of data on the diffusion of significant innovations and the judgements of technological experts.[10]

Table 5.2 Trends in per capita patenting in the United States
by major OECD countries patents per million population

	1963–68	1980–85
Japan	10.40	78.98
United States of America	236.13	157.88[a]
France	26.64	38.79
Federal Republic of Germany	55.32	97.01
Italy	8.15	14.03
Netherlands	36.61	46.89
Sweden	65.30	89.12
Switzerland	140.74	182.34
United Kingdom	44.38	40.51
Western Europe[b]	36.71	51.15

a   The differences in magnitude of per capita patenting between the USA and the other countries are an exaggeration of the differences in innovative activity as the propensity of US firms to patent in their home country is higher than that of firms from other countries.

b   Western Europe is defined as the seven European countries listed above, plus Belgium, Denmark and Ireland.

Source: OECD and SPRU/OTAF database.

Table 5.3 Sectoral patterns of relative advantage in total US patenting for some OECD countries: Revealed Technology Advantage Index

| | Chemicals | | Mechan-ical | Motor Vehicles | Raw Materials | Defence | Electrical Machinery | Electronics | |
	Fine	Other						Consumer	Capital
Japan									
1963–68	3.01	1.38	0.77	0.65	0.51	0.35	1.10	1.37	1.80
1981–86	0.87	0.96	0.81	2.08	0.40	0.11	1.11	1.71	1.86
USA									
1963–68	0.89	0.94	1.01	0.95	1.08	0.99	1.01	0.99	1.01
1981–86	0.86	0.98	1.01	0.68	1.21	1.16	1.00	0.92	0.94
France									
1963–68	1.95	0.96	1.02	1.89	0.54	1.10	1.12	1.04	0.80
1981–86	1.45	0.94	0.99	0.80	0.84	1.66	1.08	1.10	0.86
FRG									
1963–68	1.11	1.41	0.96	1.37	0.61	1.03	0.82	1.25	0.88
1981–86	1.17	1.24	1.12	1.48	0.67	1.14	0.90	0.60	0.54
Italy									
1963–68	1.21	1.66	0.95	1.01	0.76	0.78	0.68	0.64	0.36
1981–86	2.23	1.02	1.16	1.15	1.07	0.95	0.69	0.64	0.40
Netherlands									
1963–68	1.72	1.40	0.70	0.17	1.00	0.15	1.16	1.36	2.22
1981–86	0.63	1.05	0.75	0.36	1.69	0.30	1.10	1.44	1.59
Sweden									
1963–68	0.92	0.69	1.20	1.05	1.03	2.35	0.97	0.90	0.57
1981–86	0.59	0.61	1.47	0.75	1.38	2.07	0.95	0.55	0.24
Switzerland									
1963–68	2.18	1.72	0.89	0.45	0.51	1.44	0.90	0.43	0.48
1981-86	2.02	1.30	1.00	0.44	0.73	1.01	0.98	0.55	0.32
UK									
1963–68	0.88	1.00	1.06	1.55	0.65	1.28	1.04	1.06	1.09
1981-86	2.00	1.00	1.01	0.97	0.86	1.02	0.97	0.89	0.68
Western Europe									
1963–68	1.30	1.24	0.99	1.29	0.66	1.15	0.94	1.05	0.91
1981-86	1.44	1.11	1.08	1.07	0.86	1.18	0.94	0.76	0.62

a   Revealed Technology Advantage index is defined as a particular country's share of US patents within a sector divided by that country's share of total US patents. Thus a value of greater than one shows relative strength of a country in a sector and vice versa.

b   The definition of the sectors is based on an aggregation of 3-digit US patent classes, the precise correspondence being available from the authors.

Source: SPRU/OTAF database.

The dynamism of Japan

All the data confirm the considerable and growing technological strength of Japan. By the early 1970s it had already overtaken the USA and most Western European countries in firm-financed R&D as a proportion of industrial output, and by 1985 was 34 per cent above the US level (Table 5.1). The growth of Japanese patenting per capita in the USA has been even more impressive, increasing by 659 per cent between 1963 and 1968 and 1980–85 (Table 5.2). The greatest areas of technological strength have been in electronics, motor cars and marriages of the two such as robots, and of weakness in chemicals, and (not unsurprisingly) defence- and raw materials-related technologies (Table 5.3).

Attempts to explain away Japanese technological activities in terms of their low quality do not stand up to scrutiny. The explosive growth of US patenting since the early 1960s reflects the changing mix of Japanese R&D activities from the assimilative to the innovative. And two measures suggest that, by the 1980s, Japanese patenting in the USA had become of above-average quality: first, the relatively high proportion in fast-growing fields;[11] and second, the relatively high proportion that are highly cited in other US patents.[12]

The vulnerability of the USA

The technological position of the USA is no longer as strong as is often assumed. By the mid-1980s its firm-funded R&D as a proportion of industrial output was below not just Japan but also the Federal Republic of Germany, Sweden and (probably) Switzerland (Tables 5.1 and 5.2). Its sectors of greatest technological strength have over time become increasingly based on defence markets and raw materials (Table 5.3). In spite of a relatively strong position in fast-growing and highly cited US patenting, it is particularly vulnerable to Japanese technological dynamism, which has already severely affected US iron and steel, consumer electronics and motor cars, and is now affecting semiconductors, computers and telecommunications.

The variety of Europe

Generalizations about the technological position of Europe can be misleading, given the international variety in the levels and trends in aggregate technological activities (Tables 5.1 and 5.2), and in sectoral patterns of strengths and weaknesses (Table 5.3). The Federal Republic of Germany, Sweden and Switzerland are relatively strong – even up to and beyond Japanese levels; and Germany is the dominant technological power in Europe with more than 40 per cent of all European patenting in the USA in 1985. Some of the lagging European countries have had relatively rapid rates of increase in their technological activities over the past twenty years – Belgium, France and Italy; and others not – Netherlands and the UK. There is no similar pattern amongst European countries in their sectors of relative technological strength and weakness, although in aggregate, Western Europe is stronger in mechanical engineering and weak in electronics. Narin and Olivastro have pointed to the relatively low proportion of highly cited US patents from France and the Federal Republic of Germany as possible signs of low-quality technological activities.[13]

DETERMINANTS OF INTERNATIONAL DIFFERENCES

Market structure

Within mainstream industrial economics, one explanation for differing commitments to technological activities amongst sectors and countries is sought in differing industrial structures. Some argue that greater market concentration is associated with higher commitments to R&D, whilst others predict a lower commitment given less competitive pressure. And most empirical tests to determine the 'optimum' degree of concentration have used country-specific cross-sectoral data. This neglects inter-sectoral differences in technological opportunity and appropriability, which jointly determines the relationship between concentration and technological activities. Recent research has shown that, when such differences are taken into account, any relationship between technological activities and concentration disappears.[14]

Our own past comparisons of the structure of technological activities in France, the Federal Republic of Germany (West Germany) and the UK reflect a dominance of sector-specific technological factors over country-specific structural factors.[15] In spite of very different levels and trends in technological activities, all three countries have almost the same patterns of concentration of technological activities (as measured through patenting in the USA), both in aggregate and in thirty-three sectors. Thus, Figure 5.1 shows that the percentages of US patents made by the top five institutions in West Germany and the UK varies greatly amongst sectors, but that the variation in the two countries is very similar. Technological activity is concentrated in R&D-intensive sectors (chemicals, electrical-electronic, aerospace) and in motor cars, and is very dispersed in capital goods (machinery, process equipment, instrumentation).

Sector- and country-specific inducement mechanisms: factor prices, investment programmes and large firms

Given these strong inter-sectoral differences in the properties of technology, we should expect similar differences amongst sectors in the strength of the effects of country-specific inducement mechanisms on the rate and direction of technological change.[16] In particular, we identify three mechanisms:

(*i*) changing factor prices, where technological activities are undertaken to elongate what is in fact a stunted production function, in order to save on increasingly expensive factor inputs. Examples include the development of consumer durables and associated methods of labour-saving production in the USA in the 1920s; energy-efficient motor car engines developed in Western Europe and Japan;

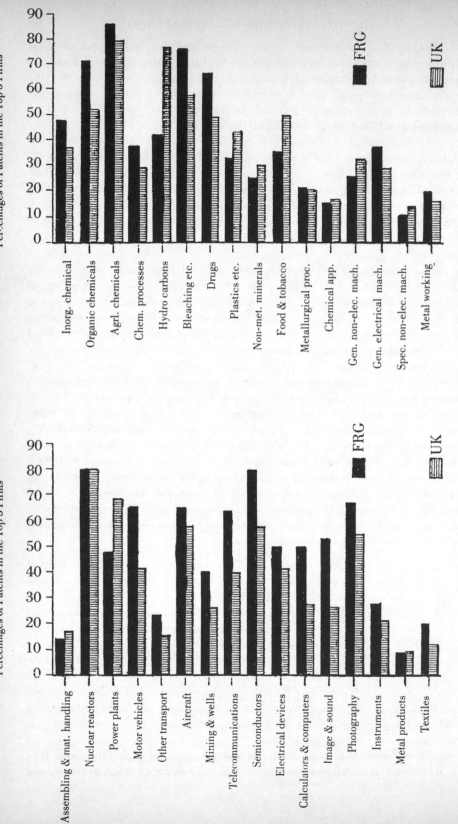

Figure 5.1 Sectoral concentration of US patenting, 1969—86

(*ii*) investment programmes (public and private) that induce technological activities in upstream capital goods, through mechanisms described by Schmookler and Rosenberg.[17] Examples include defence programmes in the USA and the UK; public investment programmes more generally in France; investment upstream and downstream of abundant raw materials in the USA; 'mechatronics' induced by investment in the automobile industry in Japan;

(*iii*) the technological activities of large firms which, as we have seen in Figure 5.1, can have a major influence on national patterns of technological activity, particularly in R&D intensive sectors and motor cars,[18] where their behaviour resembles the creative and risky entrepreneurial activities described by Schumpeter in his later writings. Examples include the large Swiss firms in fine chemicals and Philips in electronics in the Netherlands.

Dynamic versus myopic systems

However, our comparisons of West Germany, France and the UK also point to powerful, economy-wide factors influencing the propensity to innovate. In spite of very similar aggregate and sectoral structures of technological activities, West Germany outperforms the other two countries in terms of US patenting in virtually all sectors.

We have reviewed elsewhere international survey evidence on managers' opinions on the national factors influencing the propensity to innovate.[19] They identify as important the degree of emphasis on short-term profits, and the degree of involvement (and competence) of top management in determining companies' technological policies. On the basis of this and our earlier evidence, we have suggested a distinction between dynamic and myopic systems, with West Germany, Sweden, Switzerland and Japan belonging to the former category, and the UK and the USA amongst the latter.[20] Atkinson and Stiglitz made a similar distinction in 1969, and Stiglitz recently made a welcome return to the subject.[21] But there are four (not necessarily independent) reasons why firms and national systems tend to be myopic rather than dynamic:

(*i*) the system providing funding for business may evaluate mainly on the basis of short-term financial performance, in which case the cumulative and learning aspects of technological activities will be ignored;

(*ii*) as argued by Abernathy and Hayes,[22] the strict application of the managerial principles of M-form organization may stifle entrepreneurial activities, through the joint influence of using short-term financial performance to evaluate divisions, coupled with rigid definitions of each division's 'business', that effectively exclude opportunities that cut across divisional boundaries;[23]

(*iii*) firms' management may not have the appropriate mix of technological and market skills to form correct 'technological expectations' about the technological and market opportunities likely to emerge in future, as a consequence of alternative courses of action now; and

(*iv*) firms' workers may not have sufficient technical and organizational skills to enable them to accumulate knowledge at a satisfactory rate, through producing and using new technologies.

In contrast, dynamic systems tend to have business funding that gives relatively greater weight to longer term performance,[24] to have relatively more scientists and engineers in managerial positions,[25] to have labour forces with higher levels of general education coupled with stronger systems of vocational education,[26] to have higher relative levels of industry-funded R&D and of international patenting; to have greater stability in the commitment of large firms to technologies with strong potential for creating new markets and future technological opportunities coupled, with greater intra-firm flexibility to adjust organizational forms to the shape of emerging technological opportunities; and to become progressively less specialized in technologies related to specific national economic inducements, and relatively stronger in core technologies with pervasive applications.

This final prediction deserves further elaboration, since it is fundamental to the explanation of observed international differences in sectoral patterns of technological specialization. As a country develops, sectors of technological advantage will emerge through one or more country- and sector-specific inducement mechanisms, as described above. However, we would expect that, given their higher investments in technologies rich in future prospects, dynamic systems would progressively move towards excellence in technologies with potentially pervasive applications: in other words towards core fields of mechanical, electrical-electronic and chemical technologies.

The prevalence of a myopic system, rather than a dynamic one, does not necessarily preclude world technological leadership in certain sectors. The USA had such a lead in mass production, has one now in aerospace and has always had one in food and petroleum products, because of the specificities of the economic induce-ments mechanisms confronting US firms. Furthermore, US firms in other sectors have made major contributions to world technology, when they have resisted emphasis on short-term performance and the comfortable tidiness of M-form organization. Such firms have generally fallen into one of two categories. First, large firms with strong (often family) commitments to technology (e.g., Dupont and Nylon in the 1930s; Watson Junior, IBM and the computer in the 1950s; Sarnoff, RCA and colour television in the same period). Second, new technology-based firms that obtain their finance from private or local sources, and are often started by dissatisfied employees from large firms (e.g. many firms making personal computers over the past ten years). In this context, the prevalence of such new technology-based firms in the USA can be interpreted not as a sign of economic dynamism and health but of the relative inability of large firms to exploit radical and longer term technological opportunities.

CONCLUSIONS: FUTURE DIRECTIONS UNDER FREER TRADE

We began this chapter with firm evidence on the importance of international differences in technological activities in explaining international differences in economic performance. We went on to explore the nature and determinants of these international technological differences. What can we conclude about the likely effects of freer trade on technology, economic performance and relations between countries? The standard answer is that we shall live in the best (or better) of all possible worlds. More liberalization will increase the pressure of competition and consequently speed up the rate of innovation at the world technological frontier. It will also lower barriers to the rapid international diffusion of best-practice technology, and so speed up the rate of improvement in average practice. Unfortunately, things are not quite so simple.

To begin, the assumption that all (OECD) countries move tidily towards the world best-practice technology is no longer credible. It had legitimacy from 1950 to 1970, when Japan and Western Europe were recovering from the destruction of war. Since then, it has become clear that some countries have been catching up more vigorously than others, and a few have had the bad manners to overtake the previously leading country (i.e. the USA). The reasons have been identified in this chapter. The international diffusion of technology is neither automatic nor costless, but requires considerable investment in technological learning activities by the recipient country. For a variety of economic and institutional reasons, there has been uneven development amongst countries in the development of such technological activities.

This uneven development has had another effect, namely, the emergence of pressures for protection in lagging countries, and especially in the USA, which has been particularly vulnerable to the advancing sectors of Japanese technological strength (after steel, motor cars and consumer electronics, now semiconductors and electronic capital goods). Just as the UK found it difficult to accept Germany's growing technological supremacy at the beginning of this century, so the USA today has much talk about unfair practices and level playing fields, whilst tending to ignore the higher Japanese levels of expenditure on technology as a proportion of national resources shown in this chapter.

Paradoxically, such threats of protection can speed up the international diffusion of best-practice technology by encouraging leading firms to get behind emerging trade barriers through direct foreign investment and joint ventures: witness the current moves of Japanese motor cars firms into the USA and Western Europe. But doubts must remain about the extent to which such investment leads to a transfer of technology (i.e. skills to improve) rather than just technique (i.e. machines). We have shown elsewhere that large multinational firms perform most of their technological activities in their home countries, even if these are small. Belgium and Canada apart, most countries depend mainly on home-based firms for their technological activities.[27]

All this does not plead in favour of protection, quite the contrary. As Margaret Sharp has recently argued,[28] it was pressure of outside competition in the early 1980s that stimulated Europe's sleepy electronics industry, heavily protected through state markets, into radical changes in strategies and structures. She also argues that such competitive pressures were behind the development of policies for deregulation and the Single European Market. But what it *does* suggest is that the real world is more complicated, and with different chains of causation, than the ideal world. It is not one where freer trade leads to faster rates of innovation and diffusion. Instead, it begins with uneven rates of technological change between countries, resulting from different skills, institutions and practices. This creates a threat to laggard countries. The response to the threat can be positive with more vigorous technological strategies, or negative with threats of protection, or a mixture of the two. Which course eventually predominates depends in part on economic doctrine and in part on the response of key companies. It also depends on the degree of success of national policies to ensure that countries have characteristics that are dynamic rather than myopic, in the terms that we have described above. In the light of our comparisons, we are not convinced that the US response to the Japanese challenge will be any more positive than that of Western Europe.

6 Capturing value through corporate technology strategies*

David J. Teece

INTRODUCTION

Competition is essential both to the innovation process and to capitalist economic development more generally. But so is co-operation. The perennial challenge to policy-makers and to managers alike is to find the right balance of competition and co-operation, and to design the appropriate institutional structures within which competition and co-operation can take place. Today this problem has taken on a new importance, for several reasons. One is that the manner in which technological innovation is organized is changing worldwide. These changes, which will only intensify under liberalized trading regimes, relate not only to the way in which research is organized but also to the way in which new technology is acquired and commercialized. The highly stylized, linear model of innovation, with research, experimental design, development, manufacturing start-up, marketing and distribution occurring sequentially inside a single firm, has given way, particularly in some new industries, to collaborative structures among firms in which activities occur simultaneously rather than sequentially. Accordingly, corporate technology strategies are no longer simply matters of setting R&D budgets and identifying projects on which to lay bets. With an interdependent global economy, technology strategy must attend to both technology acquisition and commercialization issues.

Unfortunately, economics textbooks tell us virtually nothing about these issues. While there is usually some consideration given to the import of monopoly and competition on incentives to innovate, it is always implicitly assumed that the price mechanism can effect whatever co-ordination the economic system requires. Typically there is no discussion how inter-firm agreements, vertical, lateral and horizontal, can positively impact the process. It is not surprising, therefore, that the economics textbooks do not convey a sense that corporate technology-acquisition strategies or inter-firm co-operation are desirable, or even subjects worthy of study.[1]

Notwithstanding these limitations, the economics literature has always recognized the central importance of technological innovation to economic growth

* I am grateful to John de la Mothe and Louis Marc Ducharme for their helpful insights into corporate behaviour and market environment. Without their editorial assistance, this chapter would not have been completed.

and welfare. For example, Adam Smith's *Wealth of Nations* plunged immediately into discussions of 'improvements in machinery', and Karl Marx's model of the capitalist economy ascribed a central role to technical innovations in capital goods. Even Alfred Marshall did not hesitate to describe knowledge as the chief engine of progress in the economy. Paul Samuelson has always acknowledged the importance of technological change in his leading text, but then, like many others, he proceeds to ignore it, causing Stiglitz in the *Brookings Papers* to lament that 'while it is the dynamic properties of capitalism ... that constitute the basis of our confidence in its superiority to other forms of economic organization, the theory is based on a model that assumes an unchanging technology.[2] When technology is taken into account, the economics profession at large has, according to Nathan Rosenberg, treated it as events transpiring inside a black box, and has 'adhered rather strictly to a self-imposed ordinance not to inquire too seriously into what transpires inside that box.'[3] Therefore, it is not surprising that economists have not had much to say about corporate technology strategies and the role of co-operation. Policy analysts and policy-makers have instead both stressed the value of pluralism and rivalry as the best organizational arrangement to promote innovation.

The basic conclusion of the chapter is that co-operation will become increasingly necessary to promote competition, particularly when industries are fragmented and market barriers are low. Very few firms can successfully 'go it alone' any more. The sources of know-how are dispersed globally, and the capabilities needed to commercialize new technology are rarely found inside a single firm or a single country. Thus global co-operation among firms (and implicitly among nations) has become increasingly relevant to national economic development and growth.

Co-operation in turn requires inter-firm agreements and alliances, as well as a well-functioning price system. In this regard, the Japanese form of industrial organization, with complex inter-firm relationships, may have distinct advantages. European and US firms are now only beginning to learn how to co-operate effectively in order to compete. But as Europe approaches 1992 and as the USA and Canada become more advanced in the industry-by-industry implementation of their Free Trade Agreement (FTA), it will become more essential for innovating firms to learn when and how to co-operate in order to capture value through technological innovation.

One consequence of this adaptation to the enlarged scope of the market will be that managers must become more adept at managing inter-firm relationships. Indeed, the very concept of the corporation may well have to be reconsidered when enterprise performance is intimately linked to the performance of one's co-ventures. Similarly, at the level of public policy, technology and competition policy must be crafted so as to be sensitive to the needs of innovating firms. In some countries this is likely to require greater inter-agency co-ordination. In the USA this will need to be coupled with judicial and legislative changes that recognize that some co-operation, even among competitors, is generally beneficial when it serves the requirements of innovation.

MODELS OF CORPORATE INNOVATION, COORDINATION AND COOPERATION

At the corporate level, innovation can be seen as the search for and the discovery, development, improvement and adoption of new processes, new products, and new organizational structures and procedures. It involves risk-taking and uncertainty, and is characterized by sunk costs and strong irreversibilities.[4] Corporate innovation is also a cumulative activity that involves building on what has gone on before, whether it is inside the organization or outside the organization, whether the organization is private or public, whether the knowledge is proprietary or in the public domain.

Traditional descriptions of the corporate innovation process have commonly broken it down into a number of stages which proceed sequentially. Thus, innovation is characterized as proceeding linearly from research, to development, design, production, and then finally to marketing, sales and service. Often feedback or overlap between and among stages is not recognized. Even if this representation was once appropriate, it no longer accurately characterizes the corporate innovation, except in unusual instances.[5]

The innovation process does not necessarily begin with research; nor is it serial. Design rather than science is often at the centre. Research is often spawned by the problems associated with trying to get the design right. Moreover, technological developments draw, if necessary, on an array of sciences. Indeed, important technological breakthroughs can often proceed even when the underlying science is not understood. Products can often be made to work without much knowledge of why. The traditional linear model also underemphasizes the importance of process innovation.[6]

In corporate reality – with uncertainty, learning and short product life cycles – innovation requires rapid feedback between corporate functions, and especially between marketing, manufacturing and design. Feedback and trials are essential, especially if incremental rather than radical innovation is at issue. Indeed, incremental improvement is a large part of what corporate innovation is all about. In order to succeed at it, a team designs a new version of the product and, working closely with manufacturing and marketing, brings it to market. Speed is critical since the prior product generation is already in the market-place and typically open to reverse engineering and imitation; firms that can get out the next generation product in the shortest time are likely to expand their market share.

The firm's identification of user needs is also critical to its profitable expenditure of R&D dollars. Therefore, R&D personnel must be closely connected to the market and to marketing personnel. The corporation *in toto*, must also have a good perspective on the technological capabilities it possesses, those that it needs, and how to develop, 'rent' or buy those that it does not have. Indeed, innovation increasingly requires access to assets that are beyond the capabilities of the firm originating the innovation.

Thus successful new product and process development innovation often requires co-operation with suppliers and customers, and sometimes with firms that might be construed as competitors. Co-operation can help reduce unnecessary duplication of research efforts and can pool diverse capabilities in development and manufacturing.[7] It can also assist in the definition of technical standards in instances where systems interactions are apparent.

In view of these developments, which have now been apparent for at least two decades, the US view, at least in policy circles, is still predominantly hostile to co-operation. Europe and Japan clearly see it differently. Japanese co-operative activity is legend, and European efforts in this direction are clearly growing. Collaboration activities in Europe have already reaped manifold benefits, lessening earlier scepticism. So far the USA has been resilient to policy changes elsewhere.

The concept that is necessary for technological development must become embedded in a firm's global technology strategy if it is to compete successfully in a world where the sources of know-how are globally diffused, where imitation is often easy and where governmental barriers to trade and investment are evaporating. The following section explores how inter-firm (co-operative) agreements to access technology and complementary assets can be made an integral part of a firm's technology strategy.

COOPERATIVE DIMENSIONS OF TECHNOLOGY STRATEGY[8]

Figure 6.1 portrays three key dimensions of technology strategy. The y axis (level of R&D expenditures) is what the research manager has traditionally thought of as the key choice variable. However, as indicated earlier, there is a variety of reasons why firms must assess the particular aspects of research, development and commercialization to perform in-house, and those to perform in co-operation with other firms, domestic or foreign. (These decisions are represented by the z and x axis in Figure 6.1.) The reasons can be summarized as follows:

1. The frequency of technological discontinuities or technology paradigm shifts seems to have increased. When technological development takes a new trajectory, the direction of technical development is no longer cumulative and self-generating. Technological development then requires reference to the technical and commercial environment external to the firm. In short, the logic of previous technical advance is broken; and the capabilities that the firm possesses in-house may no longer suffice. Technological discontinuities have been a feature of technological advance since time immemorial, but according to one source they are on the increase.[9]

2. The costs of innovation have increased markedly, and the ability of a single firm to 'go it alone', particularly with respect to large systems (e.g. the Boeing 767 or the Airbus A300) may have declined. In short, even setting aside matters of risk, the financial requirements may strain even giant enterprises.

3. The sources of innovation have become more diffused internationally; thus, the probability that any one firm, even if it is a large multinational, could command all the expertise relevant for global competition even for a single product is declining. Certainly, the technological dominance of US firms in many industries has been challenged.

4. The speed with which new technologies must be commercialized has increased to the point where few firms have the time to assemble all of the requisite capabilities in-house. In part, this is because of more rapid technological change. It is also because of more rapid imitation. Accordingly, there are many cases where

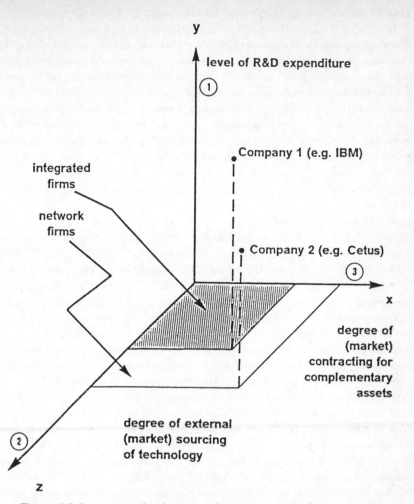

Figure 6.1 Organizational and resource dimensions of technology strategy

collaboration with other firms that already have the requisite turns out to be the dominant market entry strategy.[10]

5. For large firms, the incentive properties of small firms – and, in particular, their ability to reward innovators handsomely in ways that large established firms find difficult to replicate – favour the pursuit of technical opportunities externally.[11]

6. Liberalization of trade and investment regimes in the period since 1945 has provided firms with greater choice with respect to how technology can be developed and commercialized.

In the next three sections of this paper, global technology sourcing and commercialization strategies will be further analysed.

FACTORS IMPACTING TECHNOLOGY SOURCING STRATEGY

Whether innovating firms ought to source technology internally or externally depends on the interrelationships between three key sets of factors, each of which will be explored in turn: (*i*) the organizational location of the sources of invention/know-how; (*ii*) the ease of appropriability, i.e. whether the sponsoring firm can rely on the protection afforded by intellectual property law to capture the benefits from the research activity in question; and (*iii*) the facility with which contracts for the purchase or sale of the technology in question can be written, executed and enforced (that is, transaction costs).

Sources of know-how

Winter[12] argues that innovation involves mixing public know-how, proprietary know-how external to the firm (imitation) and internal know-how. When innovation is driven primarily by internal know-how and capabilities, a firm's ability to exploit technical opportunities is constrained primarily by its accumulated stock of proprietary know-how, its organizational and learning skills and its experience in the relevant activities. These assets take time to build and are a function of past activities in both research and production. Capabilities relevant to a particular technological paradigm over time become embedded in its research routines.[13]

The skills, know-how and experience necessary to innovate in one design paradigm, however, are usually quite different from those required in another. Thus, if a firm's established technological trajectory is particularly magnificent, or if it is able to lead the shift in an industry from one design/technological regime to another, then that firm may be able to continue relying on internal capabilities to generate relevant know-how. However, shifts in technological regimes are often propelled by firms that do not have the deepest skills in the established paradigm. Thus, when the transistor replaced the vacuum tube in the mid-1950s, vacuum-tube manufacturers were not the pioneers. Indeed, Sylvania kept investing in increasingly sophisticated vacuum-tube designs until 1968. It was an entirely new set of producers that emerged to develop and produce transistors.[14]

Hence, a shift in technological paradigms (a technological discontinuity) is likely to cause a shift in the locus of high payoff innovative efforts in ways that threaten incumbents. Incumbent firms will thus have to consider acquiring the new technology. They may be able to do so through naked imitation; however, if the innovation in question is patentable or otherwise protected, the technology may need to be purchased externally.

Note that public institutions – universities and government laboratories – may be important sources of new technology, particularly in the early stages of an industry. Inasmuch as such establishments are unable to unwilling as a matter of policy to engage in commercialization activities, the requirement and the opportunity for collaboration with established firms are provided. In these circumstances, firms – both incumbents and new business ventures – are forced to seek technology externally.

Appropriability issues

Appropriability is used here to describe the degree to which intellectual property law provides monopoly protection for a technology. When legal protection is weak, the technology may be exposed to easy imitation. Sometimes the organizational locus of innovative activity will affect the degree to which a firm can protect its technology. Thus if R&D resources, whether allocated externally or internally, can be expected to produce equally beneficial technical outcomes, appropriability concerns are likely to favour internal procurement for at least two reasons. One is the cumulative nature of learning, and its organizational setting. The procuring firm, should it 'contract out', is likely to deny itself important learning opportunities. If 'one shot' improvements along a particular technological trajectory, as with research to meet a particular fixed regulatory standard, are all that is contemplated, then permitting the developer to benefit from learning may not prevent a problem. Generally, however, future advances are contemplated, and if these can profitably build upon earlier R&D activity, internalizing the activity will be necessary. Even though the developer may pass on the benefits of past learning acquired under previous R&D contracts with the procurer, there are circumstances under which this may not occur. In-house research guards against these contingencies.

A second and related reason is that the unaffiliated developer of new products and processes is generally free to contract with other procurers. This can result in the leakage of technology developed on one company's R&D dollar to another. Internationalization forces an exclusive contract, and avoids the spillover that might otherwise occur through the R&D contracting process. Spillovers may still, of course, occur in other ways, as when R&D personnel switch employment.

The desirability of an external procurement approach increases if the sources of relevant technology are external to the firm.[15] However, even if new technology emerges elsewhere, a firm's willingness to secure a licence to use it is likely to depend on intellectual property and transaction cost considerations. If the technology is of a kind for which intellectual property law affords no protection and if copying is easy, then the acquiring firm need only imitate; no commercial transaction need result. If, on the other hand, the technology at issue is protected by patents, trade secrets and other legal structures, or is simply difficult to copy, then some kind of formal purchase contract and/or technology transfer agreement will be required.

While there are many exceptions, it is generally the case that very little know-how can be shielded effectively through patent and trade secret protection alone. One major exception is chemical-based technologies, where patent protection, due to the nature of the technology, is intrinsically stronger. Xerography and instant photography are other major exceptions. Patent protection is generally much weaker in machine and process equipment technologies because the nature of the technology makes it vulnerable to reverse engineering.[16]

If property rights are very strong, the innovator's reluctance to license is often overcome because the possibility of extracting an economic return comparable to that which could be obtained internally is increased. Conversely, when intellectual property protection is weak, new technology, if it is developed at all, will be developed internally for internal use.[17]

In short, strong patent protection allows the innovator to market its product or process innovation without exposing it to risk of imitation. In contrast, a tighter link, possibly even vertical integration, between sources and users of technology, is required when patent protection is weak. Integration, of course, enables trade secret protection to shield the technology from would-be scrutinizers of the technology. The corollary is that incumbent firms will have to come to terms with the sources of technology when the sources are external. If the appropriability regime is weak, they may simply be able to imitate. If it is strong, then imitation is less viable, and some kind of licensing arrangement may have to be sought. The viability of this depends, in turn, on transactions cost considerations, which we now examine.

Transactions costs

Transactions costs considerations lie behind the appropriability issues previously discussed. Transactions costs relate to the ease with which contracts for the purchase or sale of a commodity, in this case technology, can be written, executed and enforced without leading to unexpected outcomes that impose large costs on one or both parties.[18] In the case of technology, licence agreements are risky if one or both parties must make highly dedicated investments whose value depends on the other party's performing as anticipated.

The biggest transactional risks for the seller are associated with the buyer's using the technology in ways not anticipated by the contract, or that while anticipated cannot be easily prevented. For instance, the licensee may use the technology as a stepping stone to related technologies that are competitive with the licensor, and which cannot easily be prevented by contract. These risks are usually ameliorated if the technology has good protection under relevant intellectual property law.

The biggest risks for the buyer stem from the fact that the technology may not perform at expected levels. This problem stems from the fundamental paradox of information: one often does not know what one has purchased until after the fact.[19] In short, a buyer must typically engage in a transaction in which he has incomplete information about the commodity being purchased.[20]

Delivery is another problem. Technology must be transferred from seller to buyer for the transaction to be complete. This can be costly. Unless the technology is highly codified, transfer is likely to involve the transfer of technical personnel; and, depending on the complexities of the technology and the way in which the transfer is managed, the success of the transfer is uncertain.[21] In short, the viability of a market relationship involving technological collaboration will be driven in part by the transactions cost conditions surrounding the contract. It ought to be evident that high transactions costs will block an arrangement even when it would be warranted on other grounds. Such a condition is commonly referred to as 'market failure'. Market failures are non-events. They cause deals to be avoided because it is not possible to formulate and/or enforce a mutually acceptable arrangement between buyer and seller. The next section examines procurement strategies in light of these considerations.

SOURCING STRATEGIES

There are a number of modes by which technology lying external to the firm can be acquired. If it is easy to copy because it lacks intellectual property protection and can be reverse engineered at low cost, as with some microprocessors, then as we have seen imitation is often a viable acquisition strategy. When the technology is legally protected, is hard to copy and the innovator is willing to sell, then a number of possible contractual relationships are possible. They include licensing, contract R&D, R&D joint ventures and bilateral collaborative arrangements.

Licensing is the most familiar of these approaches. A firm possessing valuable know-how that is protected can contract to let others use the technology in question. A licence agreement will often be accompanied by a know-how agreement under which the owner of the intellectual property in question will contract to assist the buyer in developing a comprehensive understanding of the technology in question.

Contract R&D is also an important mode, though it is also fraught with hazards. When a buyer commissions R&D work to be performed under contract, it is usually in recognition of the fact that the provider of the R&D services is better positioned to generate a desirable output from R&D than is the buyer itself. Unless the technology to be developed can be specified with great precision, and the costs of the requisite development activities can be gauged with considerable accuracy, contracting to develop technology using fixed-price contracts is not easy, as it is difficult to specify and cost-out the object of the development activity at issue. Modest technological endeavours can be arranged this way more satisfactorily than can ambitious ones (that can typically be organized externally only by cost-plus contracts) but are exposed to obvious incentive hazards.

R&D joint ventures make sense as external procurement mechanisms when the other party can bring certain capabilities to the venture that the collaborating party does not possess. Other properties of joint ventures are that they reduce risk when project costs are high; and in the R&D area, they may reduce duplication without necessarily reducing variety. An inherent flaw of capitalist market economics is that they often cause patent races and other forms of socially wasteful R&D duplication. There may not be a better system for promoting innovation than capitalism, and gross inefficiencies associated with duplication can be reduced by joint ventures. Research consortia, such as the Microelectronics and Computer Corporation (MCC) formed by a group of computer companies, are an example.

Another collaborative mechanism involves bilateral exchanges of know-how and other assets, as with cross-licensing, patent-pooling and, more recently, technology transfers, in return for some other non-pecuniary commercial favour, such as access to distribution facilities. These services are often difficult to obtain otherwise, particularly under simple purchase contracts; and the reciprocal nature of collaboration can bring a degree of incentive capability and stability to the arrangement that would not otherwise be available.

The discussion so far has focused primarily on how external sources of technology can be tapped and what the role of collaborators in this process is. However, the strength of the imperative for incumbent firms – i.e. firms heavily committed to an industry – to engage in such activity is more than just a function of the attractiveness of the technological opportunities that lie external to the firm. It may also reflect the fact that failure to shape the new technology may result in the stranding of investments supporting the existing technology. Often this is unavoidable, i.e. a new technology, requiring a new set of inputs and new processing equipment, once commercialized, will destroy the value of investments supporting the existing technology. Incumbents may sometimes be completely helpless before such competitive pressures; however, in some cases, new technologies can be fashioned to deliver superior performance while still placing a demand on the investment put in place to support the old technology. In these cases, affiliation with those developing and shaping new technology has obvious advantages.

ACCESSING COMPLEMENTARY ASSETS[22]

The perspective so far has been dominated by that of incumbent firms seeking to acquire new technology that has originated elsewhere. But an equally interesting perspective is that of the developer of new technology, seeking access to the relevant 'downstream' complementary assets. In almost all cases, the successful commercialization of new technology requires that the know-how in question be utilized together with the services of other assets. Marketing, competitive manufacturing and after-sales support are always needed to commercialize successfully a new product or process. These services are often obtained from complementary assets that are specialized. For example, the commercialization of a new drug is likely to require the dissemination of information and samples over a specialized distribution channel. In some cases, the complementary assets may be the other parts of a system. For instance, hypersonic aircraft may require different landing and servicing facilities.

As a new technology paradigm is developing, usually competing designs are being worked on simultaneously. Before a dominant design emerges, there is little to be gained from firms deploying specialized assets, as scale economies are unavailable and price is not a principal competitive factor. As the leading design or designs begin to be selected by users, however, volumes increase; and opportunities for economies of scale and low-cost production will induce firms to begin gearing up for mass production by acquiring specialized tooling and equipment, and possibly specialized distribution as well. Because these investments involve significant irreversibilities, and hence risks, producers must proceed with caution.

The degree of interdependence between the innovation and the complementary assets can, of course, vary tremendously. At one extreme, the complementary assets may be virtually generic, have many potential suppliers including incumbent firms and be relatively unimportant when compared with the technological breakthrough represented by the innovation. At the other extreme, successful commercialization of the innovation may depend critically on an asset that has only one possible supplier. Such assets might be labelled 'bottleneck' assets.

Between these two extremes there is the possibility of 'co-specialization' – where the innovation and the complementary assets depend on each other. An example of this would be containerized shipping, which requires specialized trucks and terminals that can work only in conjunction with each other.

A key commercialization decision the owners of the new technology have to make is what to do (build, buy or rent) with respect to the complementary assets. Although there is a myriad of possible arrangements, two pure types stand out — namely, owning or 'renting'. At one extreme, the innovator could integrate into (i.e. build or acquire) all of the necessary complementary assets. This is likely to be unnecessary as well as prohibitively expensive. It is well to recognize that the variety of assets and competences that need to be accessed is likely to be quite large even for only modestly complex technologies like personal computers. To produce a personal computer, for instance, a company needs expertise in semiconductor technology, disk-drive technology, networking technology, keyboard technology and several others. No company has kept pace in all of these areas by itself.

At the other extreme, the innovator could attempt to access these assets through collaborative contractual relationships (e.g. component supply contracts, fabrication contracts, distribution contracts, etc.). In many instances, contracts may suffice, although a contract does expose the innovator to various hazards and dependencies that it may well wish to avoid. An analysis of the properties of the two extreme forms ought to be instructive. A brief synopsis of mixed modes then follows. The perspective adopted is that of the new entrant rather than that of the incumbent.

Contractual modes

The advantages of collaborative agreements — whereby the innovator contracts with independent suppliers, manufacturers or distributors — are fairly obvious. The innovator will not have to make the up-front capital expenditures needed to build or buy the assets in question. This reduces risks as well as cash requirements. Also, contractual relationships can bring added credibility to the innovator, especially if the innovator is relatively unknown while the contractual partner is established and viable. Indeed, arms-length contracting that embodies more than simple buy–sell agreement is becoming so common that various terms (e.g. 'strategic alliances', 'strategic partnering') have been devised to describe it. Even large companies such as IBM are now engaging in it. For IBM, partners enable the company to 'learn things [they] couldn't have learned without many years of trial and error.'[23] IBM's arrangement with Microsoft to use the latter's MS-DOS operating system of software on the IBM PC facilitated the timely introduction of IBM's personal computer into the market. Had IBM developed its own operating system, it may have missed the market window.

It is most important to recognize, however, that strategic partnering is exposed to certain hazards, particularly for the innovator and particularly when the innovator is trying to use contracts to access special capabilities. For instance, it may be difficult to induce suppliers to make costly, irreversible commitments that depend for their success on the success of the innovation. To expect suppliers, manufacturers and distributors to do so is to invite them to take risks along with the innovator. The problem that this poses for the innovator is similar to the problems associated with attracting venture capital. The innovator must persuade its prospective partner that the risk is a good one. The situation is open to opportunistic abuses on both sides. The innovator has incentives to overstate the value of the innovation, while the supplier has incentives to 'run with the technology' should the innovation be a success.

In short, the current euphoria over 'strategic partnering' may be partially misplaced. The advantages are being stressed[24] without a balanced presentation of transactional hazards. Briefly: (*i*) there is the risk that the partner will not perform according to the innovator's perception of what the contract requires; and (*ii*) there is the added danger that the partner may imitate the innovator's technology and attempt to compete with the innovator. Both problems stem from the transactions cost problems discussed earlier. The latter possibility is particularly acute if the provider of the complementary asset is uniquely situated with respect to the specialized assets in question and has the capacity to absorb and imitate the technology.

Integration modes

Integration modes, which by definition involve equity participation, are distinguished from pure contractual modes in that they typically facilitate greater control and greater access to commercial information.[25] In the case of a wholly owned asset, this is, of course, rather extensive.

Owning rather than renting the requisite specialized assets has clear advantages when the complementary assets are in fixed supply over the relevant time period. It is critical, however, that ownership be obtained before the requirements of the innovation become publicly known; otherwise, the price of the assets in question is likely to be raised. The prospective seller, realizing the value of the asset to the innovator, may well be able to extract a portion, if not all, of the profits that the innovation can generate by charging a price that reflects the value of the asset to the innovator. Such 'bottleneck' situations are not uncommon, particularly in distribution.

As a practical matter, however, an innovator may not have the time to acquire or build the complementary assets that ideally it would like to control. This is particularly true when imitation is so easy that timing becomes critical. Additionally, the innovator may simply not have the financial resources to proceed. Accordingly, innovators need to assess the importance of complementary, specialized assets. If the assets are critical, ownership is warranted, although if the firm is cash constrained, a minority position may well represent a sensible trade-off. If the complementary asset in question is technology or other personnel-related assets, this calculation may need to be revised. This is because ownership of creative enterprises appears to be fraught with hazards as integration tends to destroy incentives and culture.[26]

Needless to say, when imitation is easy, strategic moves to build or buy complementary assets that are specialized must occur with due reference to the moves of competitors. There is no point in moving to build a specialized asset, for instance, if one's imitators can do it faster and cheaper. Figure 6.2 is a simplified view of how these factors ought to condition the integration decision for a firm that does not have good intellectual property protection and does not already own the complementary assets needed to bring the new product or process to market successfully.

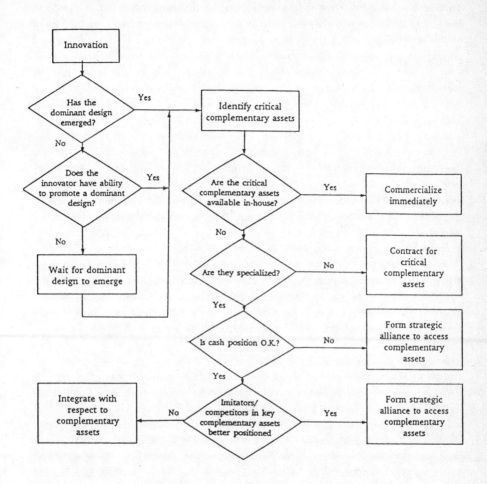

Figure 6.2 Complementary assets integration v. collaboration decision

It is self-evident that if the innovator is already a large enterprise with many of the relevant complementary assets under its control, integration is not likely to be the issue that it might otherwise be because the innovating firm will already control many of the relevant specialized and co-specialized assets. In industries experiencing rapid technological change, however, it is unlikely that a single company has the full range of expertise needed to bring advanced products to market in a timely and cost-effective fashion. Hence, integration is not just a small-firm issue.

Mixed modes

The real world rarely provides extreme or pure cases. Decisions to integrate or license involve trade-offs, compromises and mixed approaches. It is not surprising, therefore, that the real world is characterized by mixed modes of organization, involving judicious blends of contracting and integration. Relationships can be engineered around contracts in ways that are functionally akin to integration; internalization can be so decentralized that it is akin to contracts. Still, comparative analysis of the extremes can provide important insights into mixed modes.

Between the extremes of pure contracts and internal organization lies a rich diversity of governance structures that mix elements of both. We view these as an attempt to combine judiciously the flexibility of arms-length contracts with the co-ordination and communication properties of internal organization. There are various mechanisms that can be used to build such intermediate structures. Two of these, equity joint ventures and direct equity participation, are examined below.

Equity joint ventures

An equity joint venture, the creation of a new entity jointly owned and operated by the collaborators, is the classic form of organizing collaborative activity. Indeed, most studies of jointly organized activities have focused almost exclusively on this legal form. Equity joint ventures have two governance properties that make them ideal for co-ordinating complex transactions involving specialized assets. First, they create an administrative hierarchy (quite similar to internal organization) for setting general operational and strategic policies as well as for settling disputes. This hierarchical structure dispenses with the need for collaborators to attempt the often impossible task of specifying a complete set of contractual provisions for conducting the collaboration. Instead, the collaborators need only agree on a broad set of governing rules that provide a framework for deciding on more specific conditions as more information becomes available. In addition, the governing body of the venture, usually composed of representatives of both companies, provides a channel for communicating pertinent information and for co-ordinating the collaborative roles of each partner.

The second advantage of equity joint ventures is that both parties hold a direct stake (through their equity position) in the success of the project. This failure aligns incentives and can lower the risk that one party will become opportunistic. Partners pay some share of the costs of any actions they take that hurt the viability of the venture. In addition, the formal ownership structure provides each party legal rights with respect to the technology of other strategic assets contributed to, or developed by, the venture. Parties can agree at the outset about the division of assets if the venture is terminated.

Joint ventures also entail certain costs that must be recognized. Generally, they take longer to negotiate and organize than other, less hierarchical forms of governance. Given these costs, they are usually appropriate only for longer term projects that involve heavy capital or technological commitment by both parties.

Direct equity positions

An alternative to establishing a jointly owned company is for one partner to take a direct equity stake in the other. This is often used where a significant size differential exists between the collaborators, and it would be impossible for the smaller party to contribute enough equity to a jointly owned company. The direct equity approach is similar to that of equity joint ventures, although generally providing for less joint control. First, the equity stake again helps to align incentives. It safeguards the smaller partner (or investee) by creating direct costs for the investor to act opportunistically. If the inventor takes any action that hurts the investee, it will bear some portion of the resulting costs through its equity stake. Usually, at the time the equity investment is made, the parties concurrently agree on a set of longer run strategic and operational goals of the relationship. The contribution of equity helps to ensure that the investor will have an interest in ensuring that these strategic and operational goals are pursued in good faith.

Second, the direct equity stake can provide some scope for hierarchical governance (as opposed to strictly contractual governance) if it allows the investor a seat on the other company's board of directors. The goal is generally not to achieve voting power. Instead, it is to gain a direct communication channel to the highest governing level of the other partner. This ensures that the top management of the partner stays interested in the business relationship. It can also help to ensure that critical problems and issues will be brought directly to the top management rather than having to percolate up from the line managers in charge of the collaborative effort. The board position also helps information to circulate the other way, from the investee to the investor. Often, the corporate investor appoints one of its high-level executives to fill the board seat and thus provides the investee with a direct channel back to the corporate partner. Like the equity joint venture, direct equity relationships have advantages over non-equity, contractual forms of collaboration when the activities in question involve transaction-specific assets and uncertainty.

Sometimes mixed modes represent transitional phases. For instance, because of the convergence of computer and telecommunication technology, firms in each industry are discovering that they often lack the requisite technical capabilities in the other. Because the technological interdependence of the two requires collaboration among those that design different parts of the system, intense cross-boundary co-ordination and information flows are required. When separate enterprises are involved, agreement must be reached on complex protocol issues among parties that see their interests differently. Contractual difficulties can be anticipated because the selection of common technical protocols among the parties will often be followed by transaction specific investment in hardware and software.

CONCLUSIONS: TECHNOLOGY STRATEGIES WITH FREE TRADE

Corporate technological innovation requires complex forms of business organization. Because technology is traded internationally and because trade, investment and transportation barriers have been eroded in many parts of the world, innovating organizations must increasingly form linkages with suppliers and customers, and sometimes with competitors.

Advanced technological systems do not, and cannot, get crafted in splendid isolation. Moreover, the communication and co-ordination requirements will increase in complexity and variability over time. The price system alone will not suffice to achieve the necessary co-ordination. New organizational structures will need to be crafted by far-sighted managers.

The development of networks and alliance structures among firms must continue as the developments in information transfer and technology trade that have occurred are fundamental and not transient. A variety of implications flows from this, for both management practice and public policy.

Managers must become adept at managing not just their own organization but also their relationships and alliances with other firms. Very often different skills are required for each, which makes management tasks more complex and challenging. Strategic alliances also must be designed to be self-organizing. Equity can be judiciously used to anchor alliances but it need not suffice as a safeguard if inadequate in amount, and if not bolstered by other mechanisms. At present there is, however, considerable organizational learning occurring with respect to such matters, both nationally and internationally; new arrangements that are balanced and durable will undoubtedly emerge.

There is a need for both management practice and public policy to adapt to evolving global environment. In the USA, for instance, there has been a general failure to recognize the importance of co-operation. One way this has manifested itself, particularly with regards to Canada (via the Canada–USA Free Trade Agreement) and 'Europe 1992', is in an absence of government inter-agency co-ordination, with science and technology policy appearing to be weak, uncoordinated and reactionary. There is also a reluctance to clear away the roadblocks necessary to permit the private sector to forge the necessary inter-firm agreements, alliances and consortia necessary to develop and commercialize new technologies. No mechanism exists in the USA to enable trade-offs to be made between technology goals and anti-trust goals. Indeed, until a greater understanding emerges as to the organizational requirements of the innovation process, anti-trust policy in the USA is likely to remain a barrier to innovation and to national competitive performance because it will continue to generate uncertainties with respect to the legality of beneficial forms of inter-firm information sharing and co-operation.

Section 4:

Changing access to markets under free trade

7   National technology strategies[1]

Christopher T. Hill

INTRODUCTION

This chapter examines how national technology strategies may change as nations enter into regimes of freer trade, with particular attention to the US–Canadian Free Trade Agreement (FTA).

First, the general character of national technology strategies is outlined. Hypotheses are offered regarding how the effectiveness of such strategies might be affected by the degree of openness of international economic relations. A brief overview is given of events in the USA that indicate the place of technological considerations in current U.S. trade policy and administration. The chapter then addresses how the USA–Canadian FTA might affect R&D, technology development and technology strategy in the two countries. The chapter must be considered an initial exploration of the issues rather than a definitive analysis.

NATIONAL TECHNOLOGY STRATEGY

The purpose of national technology strategies

National technology strategies typically consist of an overall framework or ideology that governs the design and choice of public policy instruments for the encouragement and direction of technological change. Such strategies may be explicit and formal, or, more commonly, implicit in the collection of national policies and programmes adopted over time. Nations may have different strategies for mobilizing science and technology to address their different national goals, including economic growth and development, national security or the solution of specific national problems such as communications, the delivery of emergency services or the protection of the environment. This chapter focuses on the first of these: i.e. national strategies for mobilizing technology for economic growth and development.

Several kinds of theory underlie technology-related growth strategies. For example, welfare economics yields the theory of market failure as a rationale for public policy to encourage technological development and change. Political theory argues that those who stand to gain from the adoption of national technology policies will promote them at the expense of those who stand to lose. And, constitutional theory, at least in the USA, offers a rationale for public intervention, since one of the purposes of government is to promote the general welfare.

Having a theory-based *rationale* for national technology strategy, however, is usually insufficient to specify the nature of that strategy. One needs, in addition, a theory or at least a model of where and how the processes of technological development and technology transfer occur in order to provide a basis for effective intervention. Promotional technology strategies in most market economies are based on the assumption that technology development is primarily a private sector activity and responsibility, which government can affect on the margin by making various inputs available on more favourable terms or by changing the economic climate within which private activity occurs. However, government ordinarily has a limited role to play in actually producing new technology for purposes of economic growth and development, due both to its limited capabilities and to the generally accepted philosophical primacy of market actors. Even when market-oriented governments heavily subsidize specific industries like nuclear power and air transport, they usually contract the R&D to enterprises.

Three general constructs seem to undergird most discussions of how technology is developed. The simplest argues that new technology arises out of the direct application of new scientific advances. This is the widely discussed *linear* science-push model of the innovation process, in which basic research leads to applied research, which leads to the development of new products and processes. Another construct argues that new technology arises through the continual accumulation of marginal improvements in pre-existing products and processes. This is the model of *continuous incremental improvement*, in which competitive pressures motivate the continuous search for opportunities to improve all aspects of the technology. Yet another construct argues that new technology arises from the special insights of *entrepreneurs* who recognize a new way to marry market need and technological capability, regardless of the age or source of the capability under exploitation.

These three models suggest different technology strategies and mixes of policies, and they tend to be more or less appropriate depending upon the nation and the sector in question. Whereas a technology strategy should be compatible with the existing institutions and mechanisms of technology development in a nation's market sector, it need not – indeed should not – mirror them exactly. Instead, to the degree that the aggregate of private technology strategies is insufficient from a national point of view, then national strategy may substantially conflict with private preference if it is to be successful.

Elements of national technology strategies

Typically, national technology strategies are assembled from a combination of one or more conceptually distinctive elements. For example, government support of technology development in private firms might include both the provision of funds via direct grants and contracts, and the reduction of the effective costs of private technology development via tax preferences for R&D spending. The elements of strategy discussed here are more abstract concepts than the specific mechanisms, policies and programmes that implement the strategy and can also be considered separately from the tactics of implementation. For example, even though the US

States and the Canadian Provinces have become increasingly important and controversial actors in national technology policy, for the purposes of this discussion, the choice of national or regional levels of action is treated as a tactical rather than a strategic issue.

After briefly describing nine of the elements involved in national technology strategies, this chapter analyses how each of the elements might be affected by more open international exchange and, therefore, by changes in the size and nature of barriers to free trade.

Support basic research

This element is based on the idea that the free market offers insufficient incentives for private inquiry into fundamental understanding of the natural world, and that, as a result, the limiting factor in the ability of firms to innovate is the amount of new knowledge and information available for exploitation. The incentives are weak due to the lack of appropriability of new scientific knowledge and due to the uncertainties regarding the success, timing and utility of any particular inquiry into the unknown. Politically, the basic research strategy serves the interests of higher education and scholarship, and it minimizes the role of government in industrial affairs while subsidizing a small but important part of private technology development costs.

Support advanced education

Like basic research support, this element of technology strategy is based on the fact that firms that invest in the advanced education of their technical employees may not be able to capture the fruits of their labour in return. At the same time, it is based on the fact that the work of individual scientists and engineers may yield social benefits far greater than those that are capturable by the individual. These two 'incentive shortfalls' can be offset by public subsidies of advanced education and training. Politically, such support serves the interests of industry and the universities, as well as students.

Spin-off civilian technologies from defence and other public missions

This element is based on the recognition that, so long as national needs such as defence and environmental protection require public investment in new technology, a nation may as well attempt to reap some benefits from public investments for the private economy. A full economic rationale for this strategy also requires the identification of market failures in the private use of the technical information arising from national programmes, and such failures usually are said to result from institutional problems such as the lack of adequate intellectual property protection or bureaucratic rules against access to or effective utilization of government-generated technology and technical information. Politically, the spin-off strategy also provides incremental backing for the devotion of public resources to meeting the national need; as manifest for example, in the argument in the USA that the Strategic Defense Initiative will yield not only defensive weapons systems but also knowledge in health care and a host of other civilian areas.

Support new, small firms and individual entrepreneurs

This element is based on the recognition that small firms face entry barriers, especially if they hope to exploit a new, unproven technology. The most important of these barriers is typically limited access to capital on acceptable terms; another is limited accessibility of competitively administered government R&D contracts. Politically, small business tends to be held in high regard both because of its local base and because of the view that it is an important counter to the power of large firms.

Encourage inter-institutional co-operation in technology development
The 1980s witnessed an explosion of national programmes to facilitate, or permit, co-operation in technology development among firms, universities, government research laboratories and other institutions. The rationales for such programmes are to overcome legal and administrative barriers to otherwise desirable cooperation, to take advantage of economies of scale in joint R&D, and to overcome communication barriers among the different players in the overall innovation process. Such interaction has also served to facilitate the spin-offs discussed above, to supplement the income of universities and to mollify those who would otherwise advocate a more direct government role in funding technology development.

Financially assist individual companies in technology development
The rationale for financial assistance to individual companies to develop new technology has generally featured in arguments about the high risks and lack of appropriability of the results of new technology projects in firms, as well as about the inability of prudent firms to make long-term investments in new technology when real interest rates are high. Regardless of the economic rationales offered, firms have a financial incentive to seek assistance for technology development through political means, especially if assistance is offered indirectly via tax preferences.

Protect intellectual property
This strategy is founded on the fact that resources must usually be invested in commercially exploiting scientific and technical knowledge about the natural world, and that governments must establish and guarantee rights of ownership in new technologies if there is to be sufficient incentive for private actors to make the necessary investments in them. Intellectual property such as patents, copyrights, and trademarks does not arise 'naturally' in the market economy, and needs 'artificial' establishment by law.[2] A second rationale for the protection of intellectual property is that such rights nearly always include as a *quid pro quo* that owners disclose the nature of that property in return for the protection.

Remove barriers to technological change
Governments establish numerous policies in diverse areas, often for perfectly sound reasons, which, it is argued, negatively affect the abilities or the incentives of firms to develop or use new technologies. Technological innovation is said to be inhibited by regulatory policies in such areas as anti-trust; price and entry; government procurement; national-security-based export controls; environment, health, and safety; financial markets; terms and conditions of work; and so on.

Such policies may serve legitimate ends, from both market failure and political perspectives, but they also come into conflict with developmental technology policy. Thus, modification of basic regulatory policies, as well as modification of the ways in which they are administered, to remove unnecessary barriers to technological development are often features of national technology strategies.

Acquire foreign technology and technical information

This element can be seen as an alternative to support of basic research and/or advanced education. It is based on the premise that, at the national level, it may be more effective and efficient to seek technical information from another country than it is to develop it at home, although the effectiveness of the strategy usually is thought to require complementary capability at home to make use of the information from abroad, so that countries cannot usually manage to be totally 'free riders'. Politically, countries occasionally assert a right to foreign information access as part of the 'common heritage of mankind'. Foreign information access can also advantage domestic small and medium-sized firms in their competition with large ones that have their own resources for foreign information access.

Technology protection strategy

The technology protection strategy seeks to keep indigenously developed technology at home; to protect infant industries from foreign competition by maintaining import barriers while they develop their own technology base; or to control the importation of foreign technology so as to avoid paying excessive fees, agreeing to undesirable market limitations, or paying repeatedly for the same technology. It is based on the general notion that what is in the best interests of individual enterprises may not be in the best interest of the nation as a whole, as well as on the notion that individual firms may be unable to judge the costs and benefits of technology transactions, even to themselves, without assistance from government experts. Politically, technology protection reflects the same kinds of sectoral pressures for assistance that lead to the more usual types of trade protection, as sectors that feel themselves aggrieved are typically more focused, organized and vocal than those that would stand to lose from such protection. Technology protection may also reflect the imperfections in the international intellectual property regime.

Determining a national technology strategy

It is not the purpose of this chapter to discuss the general process of how nations evolve a national technology strategy or to suggest what kinds of national technology strategy any particular nation should adopt. However, a few general comments along those lines are in order.

Advanced industrial nations in the West typically include some aspects of all of the elements discussed above in their technology policies, explicitly or implicitly. In fact, there has been a rather notable convergence of national technology strategies, featuring the usual fads and enthusiasms.[3] There exists a cottage industry of consultants, academics and policy analysts who act as 'technology strategy transfer agents', spreading the latest ideas quickly around the globe.

This convergence of strategy has three important implications. As nations adopt similar strategies to compete in similar markets and technologies, the importance of the traditional factors in technology development will reassert itself; that is, adopting a particular strategy will, by itself, confer no relative advantage. And, as all nations adopt similar strategies, what will be important will be the *quality of implementation*, not the *content of the strategy*. Technological competitiveness will depend on good strategy, well executed, and on an appropriate balance of concern and financial support for all of the elements. Finally, the convergence of strategic understanding will force a focus on better matching of the details of strategy to national circumstances and opportunities – labour and resource endowments, consumer tastes, prior investments, and the cost and availability of investment capital will re-emerge as central factors in competitiveness.

NATIONAL TECHNOLOGY STRATEGY UNDER FREE TRADE

As a rule, each of the elements of national technology strategy discussed above is intended to strengthen the indigenous capability of the adopting nation to develop, adapt or adopt new and better technologies to enhance domestic economic performance and to strengthen the ability of domestic firms to compete internationally.

However, the effectiveness of each strategic element in strengthening a country's industries, *in comparison with those of competitor nations*, is likely to be affected by the degree to which that country's trade with other nations is influenced by policies intended to restrict the exchange of goods, services or information. In order to examine how the effectiveness of an overall national technology strategy might be affected by a move towards freer trade, the potential impact of more open international exchange on the effectiveness of each of the elements of technology strategy in creating relative competitive advantage is now considered.

Support basic research

Basic research is essentially an international activity whose very ethos demands open publication and nearly contemporaneous communication of discoveries and results to the world at large. Put another way, the external benefits of basic research do not stop at national borders. In fact, it is widely argued that any attempts to bottle up basic research and isolate it from international exchange is counterproductive to the rapid and efficient advancement of scientific understanding. The only real limitations to the open communications of basic research results are the ability of potential users to understand what is published or presented and the ever-shortening time lag in its dissemination. For this reason, some argue that firms, as well as nations, need to have some involvement in basic research activities and the associated communities in order to maintain a 'window on world science'. The implication of these characteristics of basic research is that the more open is international exchange, the less effective is a basic research strategy in creating national advantage.[4]

Support advanced education

Just like ideas, people move around the world to put their educations to work. As the USA has experienced, building a superb system of higher education encourages students from around the world to take advantage of it. Some foreign graduates choose to remain in the host country, serving as a reverse brain drain, but others return home, taking with them the new knowledge they have gained. The more open is international exchange, then, the less effective is an educational strategy in creating national advantage.

Spin-off civilian technologies from defence and other public missions

Typically, nations spend the bulk of their defence and other mission R&D funds internally, and this gives an advantage to domestic firms that seek to exploit the results of such research for commercial purposes. Making use of this strategy, however, depends not only on making spin-offs possible, but on industrial initiative in seeking to exploit them. The penumbra of secrecy and negotiated arrangements between government and industry in the national defence arena may contribute to the largely national aspects of such an enterprise. This may be offset, however, if a more open trade regime facilitates both domestic and foreign firms' access to spin offs in such areas as space, environmental protection, public transportation and energy. Thus, more open trade is likely to have relatively little impact on the effectiveness of a spin-off strategy for creating relative national advantage.

Support new, small firms and individual entrepreneurs

One of the characteristics of small firms and individual entrepreneurs is that they tend to operate in somewhat localized markets, often serving other industrial customers in the same region. For them, long-distance travel by key staff is relatively expensive and it deprives the firm of the presence of essential personnel for the duration of a trip. Except for firms near national borders or firms that supply larger firms having significant export potential, freer trade is unlikely to expand greatly the size of their effective markets. That is to say, more open trade may have little effect on firms that serve local markets. For these reasons, it is unlikely that firms from other nations will be in a position to benefit from programmes of small firm and entrepreneurial support, so the effectiveness of such a programme is likely to be relatively unaffected by the degree of openness of markets.

Encourage inter-institutional cooperation in technology development

Inter-institutional co-operation is often seen in the USA and elsewhere as a way for domestic firms to co-operate in the global competition with foreign firms. However, such co-operation usually includes an element of technical information and technology sharing among the partners – whether they be firms or universities – so, if foreign firms are permitted to participate, a consortium may prove to be an unexpectedly effective mechanism for transferring such know-how overseas. As discussed later in this chapter, access to government-sponsored or sanctioned co-operative R&D efforts has become a negotiable matter in recent international discussions of both trade and science and technology relationships. The more open is international exchange, the less effective will be the co-operative R&D approach in creating national advantage because foreign firms will be able to enhance their access to the results of such domestic co-operation.

Financially assist individual companies in technology development

Grants, tax preferences and other devices have been used to assist firms in developing new technology. Typically, although not always, direct financial assistance is limited where possible to domestic firms. On the other hand, tax preferences are usually available to all taxpayers, regardless of origin. Some nations have used assistance in technology development as an incentive to encourage foreign firms to locate there. One key question is how to treat multinational firms under grant and contract programmes intended to create national advantage, since they are typically effective international technology transfer agents. Recently, access to government programmes of technology assistance has become a negotiating point in some international trade discussions.[5] Greater openness in trade is likely to mean a somewhat reduced effectiveness of this element of technology strategy because foreign firms will have better access to the results of the research that is assisted.

Protect intellectual property

Greater and more open international commerce seems on the one hand to increase the pressure on national governments to strengthen intellectual property protection, because ownership of such property becomes more important, both to access foreign markets and to block non-complying imports. On the other hand, greater openness creates more opportunities for foreign interests to acquire and copy technologies, designs and other protected intellectual property. On balance, freer trade probably serves to enhance the effectiveness of intellectual property protection, but this conclusion is highly uncertain.

Remove barriers to technological change

Regulatory standards are often viewed by importers as non-tariff barriers to technological change and to foreign marketing if they differ from, or are more stringent than, standards in the home market. Harmonization of such standards is an important element of opening up trade internationally. Like the case of intellectual property protection, freer trade probably increases the pressures on governments to reduce barriers to innovation more quickly, on the one hand, and, on the other, to toughen them so as to substitute for tariff barriers. The overall effect of freer trade on the effectiveness of removal of such barriers in enhancing technology development is probably relatively small, and freer trade probably tends to weaken the advantage given to domestic firms, *vis-à-vis* foreign firms, in developing new technology that must meet regulatory standards.

Acquire foreign technology and technical information

Programmes to acquire foreign technology would seem to be made more effective the freer trade is, simply because the barriers to such access would be reduced. Furthermore, the larger market created by more open trade would enhance the pay-off to technical advance based on foreign technical information and technology.

Technology protection strategy

By definition, movement towards a freer trade regime would tend to make this strategy less effective, to the degree that freer trade embodies the notion of more open access to technology, or that the presence of trade competitors would enable them to acquire domestic technology more easily. Table 7.1 summarizes the expected impacts just discussed of more open trade on the effectiveness of national technology strategy elements in creating national economic advantage via technology development, adaptation and adoption.

Table 7.1 Summary of the impacts of freer trade on the effectiveness of elements of technology strategy*

Elements of national technology strategy	Expected impacts of freer trade
Basic research	Weaken
Advanced education	Weaken
Encourage spin-off	Little
New, small firms and entrepreneurs	Little
Inter-institutional co-operation	Weaken
Assist individual companies	Weaken
Intellectual property	Strengthen
Remove bariers	Weaken
Acquire foreign technology	Strengthen
Technology protection	Weaken

* Authors judgements, supported by arguments in the text. Effects will nor all be of the same quantitative importance, nor are their magnitudes well understood.

TECHNOLOGY IN U.S. TRADE POLICY

In the USA, technology is becoming steadily more important and more explicit in national trade policy, and international economic competitiveness is increasingly an important theme in technology policy. The following are some illustrations of the importance of technology in trade policy.

In the Omnibus Trade and Competitiveness Act of 1988, technology plays several important supporting roles. The 'Trade Bill' embodies the Technology Competitiveness Act, whose major provisions establish several new authorities for industrial technology assistance and technology transfer at the (newly named) National Institute of Standards and Technology ('NIST,' formerly the National Bureau of Standards). The Act also requires the President to submit a report on national policy on semiconductors, fibre optics and superconductors, and gives NIST authority to contract for studies of technology issues by the National Academies of Sciences and Engineering. The Trade Bill also establishes a process to monitor international science and technology agreements to ensure that they provide Americans the same access to R&D opportunities and facilities abroad as foreigners have. Several provisions of this Act explicitly direct that assistance and co-operation with industry be limited to 'United States businesses', and others state that the programmes under the Act should be directed towards enhancing the competitiveness of US firms.

The Trade Bill also includes a provision affecting the treatment of US-owned intellectual property in international trade. Specifically, the new law gives holders of US process patents greater legal rights to stop and/or collect damages from persons who import into the USA products produced overseas, using processes patented in the USA, without permission of the US patent holder.

The Federal Technology Transfer Act of 1986, which, among other features gives Federal laboratories the authority to enter into co-operative agreements with firms and consortia of firms for research and technology development, directs the heads of the laboratories to give preference to firms in the USA when establishing such agreements.

The Omnibus Continuing Resolution for fiscal year 1988, among its multitude of provisions, appropriated $100 million of Federal funds to assist in support of the programmes of SEMATECH, a consortium of US firms concerned with developing the next generation of process technology for the manufacture of dynamic random access memory chips, or DRAMs. The companies establishing SEMATECH have limited its membership to US firms so as to limit the immediate availability of its technologies to US producers of chips and process equipment.[6]

Recognition of the importance of technology in international negotiations on economic issues through institutional change has come somewhat more slowly, but has also begun to change in recent years. For example, the Department of State has now established a formal career path for foreign service officers who make science and technology their speciality. Also, the office of the United States Trade Representative has recently been reorganized, and it has established an Office of Services, Investment, Intellectual Property, and Science and Technology to reflect the new importance of these areas in international trade matters.

The new bilateral science and technology agreement between Japan and the USA, approved in June 1988, is much more heavily concerned with industrial research and technology than was its predecessor signed during the Carter administration.

In April 1987 President Reagan promulgated Executive Order 12591 to implement parts of the 1986 Federal Technology Transfer Act having to do with international technology information access and exchange. The Order directs the National Science Foundation and the Departments of Commerce and State to develop a central mechanism to ensure that foreign scientific and technical information is readily available to US industry.

The Japanese Technical Literature Act of 1986 gave the Department of Commerce the authority to acquire, translate, interpret and disseminate Japanese technical information to industry, academia and government laboratories, as well as to co-ordinate such activities within the Federal agencies and to survey and make reports to the Congress on the resources of the USA, public and private, to translate or otherwise access Japanese technical information.

Advancing technology is at the root of continual concern about the Export Administration Act and its implementation. Adopted to protect national security from the intended or unintended loss of militarily critical technologies to potential foreign adversaries, this Act has been frequently criticized for unnecessarily limiting the ability of US firms to sell commercial products abroad that include, or are alleged to include, elements whose export is controlled. On the other hand, a few highly publicized and significant transfers of technology to the USSR and its allies have signalled the need to maintain some degree and kind of control over such exports, and the issue has usually come down to disagreements over which technologies should be controlled and who should exercise such control.

THE US–CANADIAN FREE TRADE AGREEMENT: CONSIDERING ITS IMPACT ON NATIONAL TECHNOLOGY STRATEGY

Compared with some of the issues that have driven support for, as well as opposition to, the FTA, it appears that technology has not been a major explicit concern. For example, an official economic analysis of the FTA by the Canadian Department of Finance does not take into account changing patterns of, or changing degrees of success in, research and technology development that might flow from the FTA.[7] And an analysis of the impact of the FTA on US industry by the Congressional Research Service does not explicitly consider how technological development and change might affect industry in the long run.[8] On the other hand, concern about the future direction of technology development and transfer under the FTA is one source of disagreement about the wisdom of the Agreement, especially on the Canadian side.[9]

US–Canadian economic and technological differences

There are important differences between the USA and Canada, in terms of the scale and organization of R&D in general, and of R&D in industry in particular.[10] Canadian economic activity is frequently said to be approximately 10 per cent of that of the USA, reflecting both the relative populations and relative measures of such outcomes as gross national product. Of course, sectoral ratios may be quite different from this. Spending on R&D is one such sectoral measure; R&D spending in Canada from all sources totals approximately 5 per cent of that of the USA. The ratio of total R&D to gross domestic product is about 2.8 per cent in the USA and about 1.4 per cent in Canada. Canadian industrial R&D spending from the performer's own funds totals about 4.5 per cent of that by firms in the USA,[11,12] and nearly one-fifth of the Canadian firms' 'own' R&D funds come from their foreign affiliates.[13]

Four firms (Bell Canada, Atomic Energy of Canada, Pratt and Whitney, and IBM Canada) carry on about one-fourth of all the industrial research in Canada,[14,15] and, two of these, Pratt and Whitney and IBM, are affiliated with US multinationals. The four largest industrial research performers in the USA (General Motors, IBM, Ford Motor, and AT&T) are responsible for a similar proportion.[16] The Industrial Research Institute of the USA has well over 200 member firms that have significant R&D programmes, and *Business Week* listed 915 US performers of R&D in its 1987 compilation.[17] In 1988, over 460 US firms spent US $8 million or more of their own funds on R&D,[18] whereas only twenty-nine Canadian firms spent the equivalent amount of CAN $10 million or more.[19] The largest single R&D programme of a publicly held firm in Canada is that of Bell Canada Enterprises, whose R&D spending totalled CAN $687 million in 1987,[20] whereas General Motors is reported to have spent US $4.36 billion,[21] or about nine times as much.

R&D is organized somewhat differently in the USA and Canada, as well. Canada spends a greater proportion of its total national R&D resources in its government laboratories than does the USA − about 17 per cent[22] versus 12 per cent[23] respectively. Grants to universities and spending on R&D by industry of its own funds are both relatively smaller in Canada than in the USA. Canadian R&D is less focused on national defence than is that of the USA. Canada has somewhat less well-developed systems of venture capital and regional support for technology-based economic development (the latter are expanding rapidly, however) than the USA. Overall, Canadian R&D is both relatively smaller and more centralized than its US counterpart.

There is a much greater asymmetry in trade among the two nations. The USA and Canada are each other's largest trading partners. However, in 1987 exports to the USA accounted for approximately 17 per cent of Canadian GDP, whereas exports to Canada accounted for only 1.3 per cent of US GDP.[24] That is, bilateral trade is quantitatively much more significant for Canada than it is for the USA.

The determinants of R&D in Canada and the USA

The determinants of industrial R&D performance in the two countries have both differences and similarities. As part of an extensive econometric study of the Canadian industrial economy based on data from 1969 − admittedly somewhat dated for the present purposes − Caves and his colleagues[25] examined the determinants of R&D spending in Canada. They found that '… although the levels and characteristics of the R&D spending are very different, Canadian R&D spending behaves similarly to that of a large economy in its variation across industries'.[26] On the other hand, they came to the conclusion that, '… nearly the only sort of R&D efficiently carried on in Canada is aimed at adapting foreign technology to Canadian uses'.[27] They also noted that '… the foreign subsidiary is an accomplished practitioner of R&D (in Canada), but primarily for the adaptation of technology imported from abroad'.[28] They also argued that in a small, open economy like Canada, most new useful knowledge comes from abroad, and that domestic R&D is only efficient if it is cheaper than buying information from abroad or if it allows Canadian companies to earn profits ('rents') on its results overseas.[29]

Caves and his colleagues also discussed the factors that might lead a foreign multinational to locate R&D activity in a particular country. They noted that this decision depends on, 'the importance of the particular national market to its overall operations, the degree to which the national market was similar to or dissimilar from other major markets, and the benefits of proximity to the market for the expected success of the R&D effort'.[30] Performing R&D at an overseas branch location can facilitate effective transfer of technology from the parent and can assist in customer service, plant troubleshooting and incremental change to meet local needs. To these essentially economic arguments might be added any requirements for local performance of R&D imposed by a host country in return for access to the market or as condition of investment in the country. Multinational firms may also establish R&D facilities in another country to maintain good relations with the country's economic, political and scientific élites, or to serve as a 'listening post' from which to monitor technological developments by competitors in the country.

Larger firms stand to benefit more on average from investments in R&D than smaller firms for reasons related to both economies of scale and economies of scope. Scale economies arise from the fact that the fixed costs of an R&D investment can be spread across a larger output. Economies of scope arise from the fact that, to the degree that large size also means greater diversity of product lines, larger firms have more opportunities to find applications for R&D results than do smaller ones. These observations suggest that changes in international trading regimes that lead to consolidation and 'rationalization' of industries and firms across two nations could lead to a shift of the location of R&D to the country that hosts the larger, more diversified firms after trade is liberalized. It should be noted that this need not be the larger of the two countries, but is more likely to be the country with the greater comparative advantage in the industry.

On the other hand, under some conditions, large firms are less able than small ones to develop effectively, or to make rapid and efficient use of, new technology. The internal bureaucracy of a large firm can be a barrier to recognition of new opportunities and to implementation of those ideas, once recognized, in a timely manner. As a result, large firms frequently decentralize their R&D activities both to gain some of the advantages of smaller ones in taking risks on new technologies and to respond more quickly to local markets, constraints and opportunities. This suggests that multinational firms may adopt a strategy of placing R&D facilities in countries where they have production facilities, regardless of legal requirements of the host country or of the benefits as seen through the perspective of static comparative advantage.

Place of research and technology in the FTA

It is widely believed that the FTA would have significant impact on the structure of industry, especially in Canada, but also in some US sectors. However, despite this view, neither the agreement itself nor formal analyses of it seem to pay much heed to R&D or technology transfer, two key determinants of industry structure in the long run. Examination of the FTA[31] shows that it addresses issues of direct relevance to R&D and technology transfer in the following sections. (Provisions of the FTA not summarized here may also affect R&D and technology transfer less directly by, for example, affecting industry structure and performance, or changing the access of firms to government procurement opportunities.)

Article 304: definitions related to rules of origin

For purposes of determining whether a product meets the test of 50% cost due to production in one of the countries, this article includes 'development, design, and engineering costs' as costs that may be 'directly incurred in, or that can reasonably be allocated to, the production of goods'. For classes of goods based in part on manufacture in third countries, this provision may create an incentive to perform R&D in the producing country rather than the receiving country to help meet the origin test.

Annex 705.4, Schedule 2, paragraph B.14

This is a very specific provision requiring the inclusion of certain US government research expenditures related to wheat, oats, or barley in determining whether the level of total US government support for these grains falls equal to or less than that provided by Canada, at which time Canada will eliminate import permit requirements for those grains except under certain circumstances. It is unlikely that this provision would have a significant impact on technology development in either country.

Annex 1408 to Chapter 14 on services

This annex lists the specific services to be covered under the FTA, and it specifically lists 'Professional Services (including) Engineering … and … Scientific and technical services.' The provisions of Chapter 14 indicate an intent to remove barriers to trade in covered services, with certain exceptions. Without careful and detailed examination of existing barriers to trade in these specific services in the two nations, it is difficult to speculate on the implication of these provisions for R&D and technology.

Chapter 16: investment

This chapter is silent on the specifics of investments affecting or affected by research and technology. However, in its official preamble to the discussion of this chapter, Canada asserts that, 'The negotiation of product mandate, research and development, and technology transfer requirements with investors, however, will not be precluded.'[32] This quotation refers to the prohibition in Article 1603 of the imposition by the Parties of 'Performance Requirements' on investors of the other Party, and it appears to mean that Canada interprets the FTA as not prohibiting government participation in or requirements for 'product mandate, R&D, and technology transfer requirements.'

Article 2004: intellectual property

This article reads in its entirety, 'The Parties shall cooperate in the Uruguay Round of multilateral trade negotiations and in other international forums to improve protection of intellectual property.' Canada also notes in its official commentary[33] that the two countries 'worked on an overall framework covering the protection of intellectual property rights .... In the end, a substantive chapter was dropped.' Canada further notes that Article 2004 was adopted instead.

As can be seen from this brief summary of instances in the FTA addressing R&D or technology, these concepts are not a major feature of the proposed Agreement. The FTA would appear to leave the door open under Chapter 16 for the imposition by either of the two governments of what would amount to 'local content' rules and the like for the conduct of R&D and technology transfer, relative to residents of the other Party. Therefore, the impact of the FTA on R&D and technology transfer may well have to await any actions that the two nations might choose to take, or to undo, pursuant to this opportunity.

Impact of the FTA on technology and technology strategy

When all is said and done, it remains to be seen what impact, if any, the FTA might have on R&D and technology in either country. On the one hand, for the two economies as a whole, the expected near-term price and volume changes in trade are small, typically amounting to a few per cent at most; probably even less for the USA. On the other hand, impacts in border areas and on specific sectors may be larger.

The near-term impacts of the FTA would differ not only in size but in expected direction for different sectors. An analysis by the Congressional Research Service (CRS) anticipates that the favourable effects of the FTA on US industry would fall in such sectors as agriculture, automotive, computers and semiconductors, textiles and apparel, other manufactured products, services, banks and securities, and insurance.[34] Unfavourable impacts from the US perspective are expected for plywood, fisheries, coal, uranium and non-fuel mining. 'Neutral' impacts, or unaffected industries, would include oil, natural gas, electricity, and steel. As a broad generalization, then, the CRS analysis suggests that the USA would benefit more in manufacturing and services, while Canada would benefit in some of the extractive and natural-resources-based industries. This set of findings suggests that the agreement may play to each nation's current strengths, but that it may further disadvantage Canada *vis-à-vis* the USA in the area of advanced technologies, at least to the degree that the performance of an industry in the near term will determine its future success in technology development. An offsetting consideration, however, is that over three-quarters of all US–Canadian trade already occurs without tariffs, suggesting that the overall impact on industry and technology may be small.

What is more difficult to quantify or otherwise project is the degree to which the FTA may give greater impetus to Canadian entrepreneurs and new entrants into the game of R&D and technology-based economic development, in part due to the expectation of easier access to the large US market. This may be especially true in view of the fact that most Canadian manufacturing and advanced technology enterprises are located near the US border. In the end, effects like these may overwhelm any effects due to marginal shifts in R&D and technology transfer behaviour by large and established firms, national or multinational.

Is the concept of national technology strategy viable under free trade?

The proposed US–Canada FTA is focused largely on reducing the barriers to trade between the two nations that affect the prices of each country's goods and services in the other, and therefore the quantities of such products that are traded. Almost no attention is paid in the agreement, or in analyses of it, to the strategic importance of national policies affecting the generation and adoption of new technology. To achieve a truly open international market-place may require addressing these technology-based policies at some point in the future.

Some have pointed out that the concept of independent national fiscal or monetary policy may no longer be viable under world market integration as barriers to trade fall due to political or technological change.[35] Interdependence is a recurring theme in international affairs, and there may be no choice but to accept the reality that national technology strategies will be of limited utility in creating national advantage in the not-so-distant future. Thus, in the long run, as suggested above, having a coherent national technology strategy may be necessary, but by no means sufficient, to ensure that a country not only maintains a high standard of living but also remains strong and competitive in the economic race in which nations now find themselves.

Erecting extreme barriers to international trade might be the only theoretically available alternative to learning to live in an international economy. However, the rapid decline of such nations as Albania and China which have tried to go it alone at various times in the twentieth century; as well as the unsuccessful experiences of Venice and England, which tried to bottle up their technological advantages in centuries past,[36] shed considerable doubt on the viability of that strategy.

8 Technology policy in Europe

Roy Rothwell and Mark Dodgson

INTRODUCTION

Despite national differences in approach to policy formulation and implementation, and despite differences in the perceived role of the state in influencing the rate and direction of industrial technological change, during the 1980s there was some convergence in the types of policy adopted in major European advanced market economies. Today in most countries, major national programmes exist which focus on pre-competitive inter-firm collaborative research in information technology; there is a growing emphasis on measures to assist New Technology Based Firm (NTBF) start-ups; and there is a marked trend towards measures to create technology transfer infrastructures in the less-developed regions.

In the case of private sector policies, the situation is much more heterogeneous. However, some general trends can be discerned. Following a period of retrenchment and rationalization during the 1970s, many companies during the 1980s put increased emphasis on technological accumulation and on the formulation of technology strategies as a core component of overall corporate strategy. During the same period there was a significant increase in national and international corporate alliances and joint ventures which centred on the development of key technologies and high-tech products.

Thus, to some extent, public policy developments have paralleled, and in some cases influenced, strategic technological developments in the private sector. This is particularly the case with technology policies promulgated by the European Commission (EC) in Brussels which mandates trans-national cooperation between companies. Some trends in national and EC technology policies are described below, as are their implications for '1992'.

NATIONAL TECHNOLOGY POLICIES IN EUROPE

It is no simple task to describe in any precise and detailed manner common threads in the evolution of public policies in Europe directed towards stimulating the development and commercialization of technologies. Historically, European governments have adopted quite different approaches to technology development policies, both in terms of the type of policy instruments adopted and the role the state plays in funding and directing industrial technological change. The situation is further complicated by the fact that, even in individual countries, the nature and

Table 8.1 Evolution of public research and technology development policies

1950s and 1960s	*Science policy*	*Industrial policy*	*Firm size emphasis*

	– Scientific education
	– University research
	– Basic research in
	  government laboratories
		– Grants for R&D
		- Equipment grants
		– Industrial restructuring
		– Support for collective
		  industrial research
		– Technical education
		  and training
			– Emphasis on large firms
			  and industrial
			  agglomeration
			– Creating national
			  flagship companies
			– Public R&D funds go
			  mainly to large
			  companies
			– Paucity of venture
			  capital

Little co-ordination or active collaboration between science policy-makers and industrial policy-makers

Mid-1970s to early-1980s		*Innovation policy*	

	– As above
	– Some concern over lack
	  of university-industry
	  linkages
		– Grants for innovation
		– Involving collective
		  research institutes in
		  product development
		– Innovation-stimulating
		  public procurement
			– Increasing interest in
			  small and medium
			  sized firms (SMFs)
			– Many measures
			  introduced to support
			  innovation in SMFs
			– Continuing paucity
			  of venture capital

Increasing interdepartmental co-ordination

Early-1980s to date		*Technology policy*	

	– Increased emphasis on
	  stimulating university-
	  industry linkages
	– Increased emphasis on
	  strategic research in
	  universities
		– Selection and support
		  of generic technologies
		– Growth in European
		  policies of collaboration
		  in pre-competitive
		  research
		– Emphasis on inter-
		  company collaboration
			– Emphasis on the
			  creation of new tech-
			  nology-based firms
			– Growth availability of
			  venture capital

Interdepartmental initiatives

Growing interest in accountability and in measures for evaluating the effectiveness of Public R&D policies

Increasing concern over growing regional economic disparities. National and local government initiatives to enhance the R&D potential of the less developed regions: accelerated establishment of regional technology infrastructures, e.g. science parks, technopoles, innovation centres.

Data Sources: R. Rothwell and W. Zegveld, *Reindustrialization and Technology*, Longman, Harlow, 1985; R. Rothwell 'Preface' to 'Technology Policy', Special Issue of *Technovation*, 5, February 1987

direction of governmental involvement can change considerably according to the philosophy of the political party in power.

A major difference in approach to technology development policies is the role that government plays in the economy and in industrial development generally. During the early 1980s, these differences were summarized as follows:[1]

In some countries state intervention in industry is seen as a major part of a process of indicative planning. This is the case in countries like, for example, France and Italy, where industrial policy is used as an important instrument for economic policy and where the objectives of that policy are formulated within the framework of economic and social development plans which are indicative for the private sector. Industrial innovation policy is then formulated through consultative and co-ordinative procedures and institutions within government and between government and industry.

In other countries industrial (innovation) policy is seen as part of a general economic policy, aiming to create a favourable climate for industrial development. Although these countries, like the Netherlands, Denmark and the Federal Republic of Germany (West Germany), use industrial policy instruments or even sectoral policies, these policies are not formulated within the framework of a National Plan nor are they used as selective policies in an intensive or systematic way.

Today, it is probably in the UK that the latter policy approach is most clearly articulated. UK public policy is very much directed towards creating an environment conducive to industrial development; essentially these policies are *hands-off* in nature and have focused on areas such as tax reduction, deregulation, de-nationalization and the stimulation of a viable venture capital industry.

Despite these national differences in approach to policy formulation and implementation, some rather general policy trends in Europe during the past thirty or so years can be discerned, and these are summarized in Table 8.1. Essentially, during the 1950s and 1960s, there was little co-ordination between science policies and industrial policies; the bulk of public funds for industrial R&D went to large companies, often in support of prestigious or lobby projects with questionable commercial potential; and in most countries, with a few notable exceptions such as Denmark, the small firm sector was neglected.

From the mid-to-late 1970s, increasing attention was paid to the small firm sector and many measures were introduced to assist small firms in their innovatory activities; a number of interdepartmental initiatives were introduced which linked more closely the universities with industry; and innovations which linked were introduced that went beyond simply supporting the R&D end of the innovation process.[2]

From the early 1980s onwards, European governments increasingly began to appreciate the potential economic importance of emerging generic technologies, most notably information technology (IT) and biotechnology (BT). This led to the widespread introduction of national technology policies and the emergence of trans-European technology policies under the aegis of the EC in Brussels. As part of this growing focus on generic technologies, increased emphasis was given selectively to supporting *strategic* research in universities, and to forging links between universities and companies and between companies. This was based, at least partially, on the recognition that two important features of IT and BT are as follows:

(*i*) Interdisciplinarity: to some extent they cut across established academic and industrial boundaries; and their

(*ii*) Close links with basic research: academic research in these areas is of considerable strategic importance to industry. In some areas, the time-lag between academic publication and patenting is shortening rapidly.

In parallel with the introduction of national technology policies, increasing emphasis has been placed on stimulating the creation of small and new technology-based firms (NTBFs). These are seen as potentially efficient wealth and employment creators and as vehicles for stimulating the industrial application of generic technologies. A major feature of public policy in this area has been the stimulation of national venture capital industries (as well as the creation of a European Venture Capital Association). In addition, several European countries have taken steps to establish secondary stock markets which, it is believed, act both to lower the entry barriers to NTBFs and provide a more accessible exit mechanism for venture capital investors, more readily enabling them to realize a capital gain.

Table 8.2 provides brief details on the estimated size of the venture capital industries in nine European countries (along with Japan and the USA) in 1985–86. Given that in most of these European countries there was a virtual absence of a professional venture capital sector before 1980, these data suggest high growth rates in all the European countries listed. Indeed, during 1987, total European venture capital grew at an estimated 40 per cent.

Table 8.2 Estimated size of national venture capital (1985–86)

Country	Number of venture capital firms	Total venture capital pool ($m)
UK	110	4,500
France	45	750
Netherlands	40	650
West Germany	25	500
Denmark	14	120
Ireland	10	100
Sweden	31	325
Austria	11	50
Norway	35	185
Japan	44	1,000
USA	550	20,000

Source: Financial Times, 8 October 1986

During 1985–86 the European venture capital pool totalled about a third of that in the USA. Unlike the bulk of its European counterpart, however, US venture capital is very much *hands-on*, and is supported through considerable accumulated evaluation and management expertise and efficient informal inter-fund communication networks.

During 1985 the UK venture capital pool represented about 40 per cent of Western Europe's combined pool of venture capital (£4.758 million). This owes a great deal to two public policy initiatives in the UK, the Business Expansion Scheme (BES) and the Unlisted Securities Market (USM). The BES was instrumental in the establishment of an independent (non-institutional) British venture capital industry (Small Business Research Trust). It is a scheme based on offering tax relief to individuals on investments up to 40,000 in unlisted companies for a period of five years, after which capital gains are free from capital gains tax. In 1984–85, BES-generated funds accounted for 20 per cent of total venture capital commitments and BES-related funds represented some 40 per cent of all independent UK-managed funds then in operation. Between 1982 and 1985, private investors under BES provided about 20 per cent of all funds raised by independent venture capital firms. About 66 per cent of BES funds went to firms less than five years old.

The BES scheme, of course, is an *indirect* policy tool which fits well the philosophy of the current Conservative administration. While there still remains a seed capital gap for small ventures requiring £50,000 or less, BES loans have on average been lower (£160,000)[3] than those awarded under non-BES funds (£265,000).[4]

Despite some problems – most notably a lack of targeting of BES funds on manufacturing – the scheme has played an important part in the rapidly developing *new wave* independent UK venture capital industry. In the first place, it has underwritten the entry costs to the venture capitalists, effectively reducing their financial risks. Second, it has biased investments towards early stage – and probably therefore higher risk – financing. And third, and perhaps most importantly, it has helped to create in the UK a growing body of experienced venture capital managers.[5] As of December 1985, the failure rate for BES ventures funded in 1983–84 was about 14 per cent.

The second initiative, the establishment in 1980 of the USM, also provided considerable stimulus to the growth in new venture capital funds. Between 1980 and 1984 the USM had about 250 companies quoted with an aggregate market capitalization of £3 billion, and this despite the fact that BES-based ventures had yet to be allowed access. In contrast, in the previous five years, there were only sixty new quotations on the UK stock market. The USM provided an *accessible* exit mechanism for UK venture capitalists, more readily enabling them to realize a capital gain on their investments than was the case when companies had to grow to sufficient stature to enable them to obtain a full quotation on the stock exchange.

Before the 1980s, NTBF start-up on an appreciable scale was regarded in Europe as a uniquely US phenomenon and the role that NTBFs played in the emergence and diffusion of new technologies, e.g. semiconductors and computer-aided designs in the USA was widely acknowledged. During the 1980s a number of changes occurred in Europe which considerably enhanced the possibilities for increased NTBF formation. For example, greater support was forthcoming from governments; displacement effects were brought about through company closures and rationalizations; government pressures forced academics to adopt more entrepreneurial attitudes; information technology and biotechnology opened up many techno-market niches suitable for exploitation by small firms; and attitudes in society changed more in favour of industry as a vehicle for employment creation and for wealth creation to support social services. At the same time new and enhanced technological infrastructures were created, offering better facilities and support to NTBFs. Paralleling these positive trends was the development of European venture capital as a crucial enabling factor in NTBF formation and growth. Particularly in the UK the term *enterprise culture* has become common currency and the Department of Trade and Industry small firm support schemes have for several years been promulgated under the so-called *enterprise initiative*.

It is at least partly due to the success of these factors that, during the 1980s, there has been rapid growth in the rate of NTBF creation in the UK. This is illustrated in Table 8.3, which summarizes the results of two studies on NTBFs in the UK (and West Germany), one completed in 1976[6] and one completed in 1986.[7] Following an initiative by the EC, the European Venture Capital Association (EVCA) was launched in Brussels in 1983, which included venture capital companies with total portfolio investments of about $870 million. The EVCA was intended to facilitate cross-national flows of venture capital in Europe. An important feature of the EVCA is that it creates a mechanism for trans-national information exchange, linking together venture capital institutions to provide better foreign market intelligence for national clients, thereby increasing the possibility for international joint ventures. This is a promising initiative in the context of the *single market* of 1992.

Table 8.3 NTBFs in the UK: 1975 and 1985

A.D. Little Study (1977)		Segal Quince and ISI Institute Study (1986)	
Number in existence:	200	Number in existence:	6,000 – 7,000
Total employment:	15,000	Start-up rate:	'Explosive since the mid-1970s. Most are 'very young' – post 1979.
Total annual sales (1975):	£200 million (50% from 4 companies)	Employment (1985) sectors:	About 120,000 electronics; computer hardware and software; instruments; (recently) biotechnology
Export ratio:	30%		
Sectors:	Mainly electrical		

Despite the overall increase in venture capital in Europe, there still exists a paucity of capital to fund start-ups, the so-called *seed capital gap*. For example, in 1985, seed capital as a percentage of total venture capital was 1.4 per cent, 9.6 per cent and 3.0 per cent in the UK, West Germany and France respectively. Partly in response to this problem, several European governments have developed schemes which in many respects were devised to emulate the successful Small Business Innovation Research (SBIR) Programme in the USA. For example, in 1986 the DTI in the UK announced the two-stage Small Firms Merit Award for Research and Technology (SMART) scheme, with an allocation of a budget below 1 million; and in 1983 the West German government introduced the three-phase Support of New Technology-Based Firms scheme, with an initial budget of DM325 million for the period up to 1986.

Alongside schemes designed to stimulate venture capital growth, during the 1980s European governments have introduced major national programmes for the development of generic technologies, most notably information technology. The development of national technology policies in Europe was triggered by the announcement in 1981 of the Japanese Fifth Generation Computer Development Project (5G). This represented an explicit attempt on the part of the Japanese to shift away from a technology-follower mode and to leap ahead of its Western rivals in the vital area of artificial intelligence. As indicated in Table 8.1, a major feature of these national technology programmes is their emphasis on pre-competitive research collaboration between companies and between companies and universities. Below we describe IT programmes in the UK, France and West Germany since it is these three leading European nations that such policies have been most clearly articulated and developed.

The UK government's response to the unveiling of Japan's 5G programme was the establishment of the Alvey Committee on advanced information technology, which produced the so-called Alvey Report in 1982. The Alvey Committee identified a number of main priority areas in which the UK should build up technical strengths as a basis for commercial exploitation. These major *enabling technologies* are software engineering, very large scale integration (VLSI), intelligent knowledge-based systems (IKBS) and the man-machine interface (MMI). The Alvey Programme cost 350 million over five years. Of this, 200 million was committed by the government, with participating companies providing the remainder. Government funds were intended to cover 90 per cent of the costs of projects in which wide and open dissemination of research results is required and 50 per cent of the cost of other projects. The main aim of the Alvey Programme was to facilitate inter-firm and industry—university collaboration at the pre-competitive research stage, leaving commercial exploitation in the hands of individual companies. In order to facilitate collaboration between the different institutions involved and to co-ordinate the various projects (i.e. to achieve programme coherence), a new directorate, the Alvey Directorate, was established within the DTI. In addition, independent academic research groups were given the task of evaluating the effectiveness of the Alvey Programme on a continuing basis. While it is too early to judge the success of Alvey in terms of new product introductions, a number of the benefits occurring from the participation are given later. Perhaps, in the longer term, the main benefits will be behavioural rather than technical, in the sense that Alvey participants, both companies and universities, have discovered the benefits to be gained from research collaboration and how better to manage the collaborative process.

In France, the government responded to the Japanese 5G programme by establishing the Farnous Commission (La Mission Filière Électronique) to identify the specific needs of the electronics industry, in September 1982. The Farnous Report, published in March 1982, formed the basis for the Programme d'Action pour la Filière Électronique (PAFE, announced in July 1982. According to President Mitterand, the prime aim of PAFE was to place France on an equal technological footing with the USA and Japan. Outlined in PAFE was a total expenditure of FF140 billion between 1982 and 1987, with FF60 billion of this deriving from government sources (Ministries of Defence, PTT and Industry and Research). PAFE was designed to tackle four main areas of policy intervention; research, education, industry and microelectronics applications, in a co-ordinated manner. Of the total financial allocation, 40 per cent was to go towards developments in telecommunications and professional electronics and 43 per cent to components, consumer electronics and information. The first seven projects launched under PAFE were in the areas of microcomputers, large computers, CAD for VLSI, software engineering, CAD CAM, computer assisted translation and image processing.

While Guy and Arnold[8] suggest that the restructuring of the IT industry in France associated with the PAFE programme has been an apparent success, according to them this should not:

> cloud the fact that implementation of the filière framework in which it was conceived has not been totally successful. In principle, policy measures affecting one part of a filière can have impacts on other parts. In practice, the adoption of thinking about filières and its application to industrial policy has tended to involve the treatment of filières as industries, rather conventionally understood, and has failed to exploit the policy implication of the original analysis: that by interfering in a relatively small way at one point of the filière it is possible to affect the characteristics of the filière as a whole in rather larger ways. Successful coupling on the demand − and supply − side components of the filière approach has also been hindered by the existence of a plethora of agencies dealing with individual elements of a master plan characterized more by an ethereal rather than by a corporeal nature.[9]

In 1984, in West Germany, the Kohl administration announced a four-year programme in information technology with a total financial allocation of DM3 billion. Unlike previous Federal initiatives in the electronics/information technology area, the new Informationstechnik Programme represented a more unified approach, and, for the first time, involved the co-ordination of funding between the Bundesministerium Fur Forschung und Technologie, the Bundespost and the Economics Ministry.

Many of the projects previously funded by the BMT and other government agencies have been continued under the umbrella of the Informationstechnik Programme, and the amount of extra money involved appears to have been modest. However, the degree of co-ordination between the existing projects, and between projects subsequently initiated under the programme, has been increased significantly. As with previous public policy initiatives, the Informationstechnik Programme emphasized technology diffusion of sectors of traditional German competitive strength. It emphasized in addition the use of public procurement to stimulate innovation and it aimed to stimulate the involvement of small- and medium-sized companies. The main areas covered by the new programme were components (including submicron technology and integrated optics), data processing (including new computer structures and software), industrial automation (including robotics and FMS), telecommunications (including optical technology and broadband networks), improving the research infrastructure (research networks) and education. Guy and Arnold[10] consider that the emphasis placed in the Informationstechnik Programme on diffusion research has both strengthened the user sector and stimulated the supply (IT) sector. They do, however, question the extent to which the German programme has succeeded in its intentions to integrate the various support initiatives.

Despite the convergence in the use of technology policies in the UK, France and West Germany, some differences in policy emphasis are evident, and the size, form and organization of the three programmes vary considerably. These differences are illustrated in Table 8.4. Table 8.4 shows that the French programmes was by far the largest, but that the British had a stronger focus on basic research than the French, which was more developmental in character. The British Alvey programme was strongly technology-pushed with few overt market linkages; the French PAFE programme had strong downstream linkages with telecommunications, which was seen as the core *carrier* sector for the new technology; the Germany programme not only had strong links with the telecommunications sector but also laid considerable emphasis on the diffusion of IT on existing sectors in which Germany has strong competitive strengths, and in this respect it was strongly market-linked.

Table 8.4 Government IT programmes in Europe in 1984

	Size (ECU m)	Basic research	Applied research	Tech. pushed	Market-linked	Technological and programme novelty
UK	285	25%	75%	High	Overtly Few links	High Radical technologies New initiatives
France	824	8%	92%	Medium	Strongly with telecomms	Medium Some radical technologies Filière approach continues
FRG	236	–	–	Low	Strongly with telecomms Diffusion oriented	Lower Existing projects coordinated with new interministerial umbrella

Source: Adapted from Mackintosh International (1984), Arnold and Guy (1985).

In terms of programme *novelty*, the British programme ranked highly on two counts; it focused on four radical new technologies and it represented a new style of initiative for the UK. While the French programme also tackled a number of radical technologies, it continued the well-established filière approach to technology development. In technological terms the German programme represented mainly a re-packaging of existing projects, but it did so under a co-ordinating inter-ministerial umbrella, which was a departure within the West German policy system.

Alongside the development of national programmes of collaborative pre-competitive research, the EC has, during the 1980s, established a number of community-wide technology development programmes. In the IT area, the main EC programme is the European Strategic Programme for Research and Development in Information Technology (ESPRIT), which was approved in February 1984 with a five-year budget of 1.5 billion ECUs (about $1.25 billion). Under the programme, 50 per cent of finance is derived from the EC and 50 per cent from participating companies. The four main aims of ESPRIT are:

to ensure that research teams achieved the critical mass to obtain results;
to enable optimization of resources that would result in reducing duplication and widen the spectrum of research tackled;
to reduce the time lag effect caused by reliance on imported technology; and
to pave the way to the definition and adoption of standards of European origin.

The programme included five areas of technology: advanced microelectronics, software technology; advanced information processing; office automation; and computer-integrated flexible manufacturing. Central to ESPRIT was its focus on pre-competitive research and a fundamental criterion for participation was a cross-national partnership between two research groups, one of which must be commercially oriented. According to Sharp:

Symbolically ESPRIT has been of far greater importance than either its expenditures (which at approximately 200 million a year to date have been less than most governments have been putting in their information technology sectors), on the specific projects, would imply. Concentrating, as it has in Phase I, on pre-competitive research, the emphasis has been less on products that can be brought to market rather than on the development of tools and techniques to enable such products to be developed. There have been successes, prime amongst which is the use of the INMOS transputer in the Paroys supercomputer developed jointly with the French; but one of its main achievements has been in the field of standards where work on developing software standards for manufacturing and office systems has been invaluable in opening national markets of other European manufacturers.[11]

This suggests that the standards developing activities of EC programmes such as ESPRIT will go some way towards facilitating the free flow of advanced technology products within Europe following market liberalization in 1992.

The Single European Act of 1987 – designed to speed up European integration – included as an aim the establishment of a European Research and Technology Community. The Single Act gives the EC powers in the field of scientific and technological co-operation, and forms the basis for the Framework Programme on research and development (1987–91) which is the general instrument for the EC's

Table 8.5 Breakdown of amount deemed necessary to implement the 1987–91 Framework Programme: million ECU

	EC figures	Sub-total
Quality of life		375
– Health	80	
– Radiation protection	34	
– Environment	261	
Towards a single market and an information and communications society		2275
– Information technology (ESPRIT)	1600	
– Telecommunications (RACE)	550	
– New services of common interest (including transport)	125	
Modernization of industrial sectors		
– Science and technology (manufacturing industry) (BRITE)	400	
– Science and technology (advanced materials)	220	
– Raw materials and recycling	45	
– Technical standards, measurement methods and reference materials	180	
Exploitation and optimum use of biological resources	280	
– Biotechnology	120	
– Agro-industrial technologies	105	
– Competitiveness of agriculture and management of agricultural resources	55	
Energy		1173
– Fission: nuclear safety	440	
– Controlled thermonuclear fusion	611	
– Non-nuclear energy sources and rational use of energy	122	
Science and technology for development		80
Exploitation of the sea bed and use of marine resources		80
– Marine science and technology	50	
– Fisheries	30	
Improvement of European		288
– Stimulation, enhancement and use of human resources	180	
– Use of major installations	30	
– Forecasting and assessment and other backup measures	23	
– Dissemination and utilization of scientific and technical research results	55	
Total		5396
Research programmes already adopted or in hand		+ 1084
Total		**6480**

Source: EC Bulletin, September 1987

Table 8.6 Sample of Major EC Programmes

Programme	Dates	Budget	Focus
BAP (Biotechnology Action Programme)	1986–91	75mECU	Biotechnology research related to Agro-Industries and Agriculture
ESPRIT 1 (European Strategic Programme for R&D in IT)	1984–93	750 mECU	Collaboration between independent industrial partners from two different member states in: VLSI, software development, office systems, CIM
ESPRIT 2		1600 mECU	Microelectronics and peripherals, information processing systems and IT applications. Special emphasis on applications technology and on technology transfer
RACE (R&D in Advanced Communications Technology)	(definition stage) – 1985–87	40 mECU	Theoretical and assessment work concerning development of Integrated Broadband Communications based on ISDN
	(phase 1) – 1987–91	550 mECU	Development of ISDN using broadband technology
	1987–	20mECU	Development of new technological methods of supporting school and professional education
DELTA (Development of European Learning through Technological Advance)			
BRITE/EURAM[a] (Basic Research in Industrial Technologies for Europe/European R&D for Advanced Materials)	1985–	439mECU	Applications of new technologies and advanced materials in traditional industries
COMETT (Communication Action Programme in Education and Training for Technology)	1986–90	80mECU	Development of university–industry co-operation for training and education in new and existing technologies
COMETT II*		250 mECU	

* Yet to receive final approval
Source: Andre (1988) and other EC sources

activities in this field. The EC's activities centre on a few major topics (IT, telecommunications, energy, etc.), and its policy is: 'Not to transfer to community level as much scientific and technical work as possible but to concentrate on those activities in the Member States in which European co-operation offers obvious advantages and will generate a maximum of beneficial effects.' [12] Table 8.5 gives a breakdown by field of the amounts deemed necessary to implement the various targets of the Framework Programme. [13]

Some of the ECs Programmes are summarized in Table 8.6. In the BT field, they include the Biomolecular Engineering Programme (BEP), launched in 1982, which had a total expenditure of only 15 million ECU; while its successor, the Biotechnology Action Programme (BAP), launched in 1986, has a much larger budget of 50 million ECU. [14,15]

In essence, the main problems being tackled by existing European technology policies are:

lack of inter-firm collaboration;
duplication in R&D;
fragmented and uncoordinated R&D efforts; and
too few university–industry linkages.

REGIONAL TECHNOLOGY DEVELOPMENT PROGRAMMES

The traditional instrument of regional policy in most European countries has been the use of financial incentives for companies, both national and foreign, to locate manufacturing capacity in the designated development regions. These policies were strongly social in orientation (employment creation) rather than technology-development oriented. They led to the establishment of branch plant economies in the development regions with a largely blue-collar workforce, with few strategic management or technological skills being relocated from the main centres of decision-making, R&D and production in the developed regions. More recently, policies have shifted towards enhancing the indigenous technological potential of the regions, largely through the development and enhancement of regional technological infrastructures. [16] However, regional technology policies are much better developed and more comprehensive in some countries than in others.

In the UK, where regional technology policy was late to develop, one of the main provisions of a recent White Paper on DTI reorganization with regard to innovation, is that: 'Greater emphasis will be placed on technology transfer – especially thinking educational institutions and industry – for small firms, for the regions and for new technologies' (CM278). The principal mechanism for encouraging technology transfer at the regional level is the recently established Regional Technology Centres, established under the DTI's Local Collaborative Programme announced in 1986. Thirteen centres have been, or are in the process of being, approved. Essentially, the centres are based on regional consortia of higher educational institutions with a network of private and public sector collaborative partners, including manufacturing companies, public utilities and banks.

The overall aims of the RTC Networks are to:

establish a system of collaborative centres both in the sense of individual groupings or consortia and throughout the network itself;

offer a range of technology transfer services based on training of related delivery mechanisms on a self-primary basis; and

create a highly flexible and responsive initiative that will develop on the basis of experience.

In addition, there are three well-established regional development agencies in the UK. These are the Scottish Development Agency, the Welsh Development Agency and the Industrial Development Board of Northern Ireland. All three are heavily involved in stimulating technological development and technology transfer in their respective regions, as well as stimulating the local development of local venture capital and new company start-up.

During the 1980s there was rapid growth in the establishment of science parks in the UK, which have implications for technological development in the regions in which they are located. While these were not the result of deliberate public policy, there seems little doubt that such initiatives were powerfully assisted by government cutbacks in academic funding. While only three science parks were in operation in 1980, by 1986 there were twenty-eight, with seven under construction and seven at the initial planning stage.[17]

While science parks in the 1970s were funded mainly by academic institutions, between 1982 and 1984 local authorities and development agencies played the dominant role in funding the ten parks created during that period. According to one report,[18] of the £36.5 million expended on infrastructure and buildings on science parks developed or under construction between 1982 and 1985, 18 per cent derived from private developers, 16 per cent from tenants and 11 per cent from universities. By far the largest proportion (55 per cent) derived from public sector authorities: Scottish Development Agency £5.0 million; local authorities £7.6 million; English Estates £6.4 million and the Welsh Development Agency £1.3 million.

In France, despite the dominant role of public R&D expenditures and nationalized industry R&D in total R&D expenditure, since the end of the 1970s there has been a significant movement towards decentralization (regionalization) in the provision of services via publically funded R&D institutions. During the 1980s in particular, the French government has laid considerable emphasis on developing regional ST&T policies, with a strong emphasis on the small- and medium-sized firms (SMF) sector. For example, the Agence Nationale pour la Valorisation de la Recherche (ANVAR), which was constituted in 1968 to assist laboratories, in particular public laboratories, in licensing patents, was restructured in 1978 and now has twenty-two regional offices. These have local decision-making autonomy in providing financial assistance to SMFs under the Innovation Aid Financing Programme. Similarly, in the case of the Centre National de la Recherche Scientifique (CNRS) (the principal organization in France for fundamental scientific research), an active programme of regionalization is underway. In support of regionalization, CNRS is regrouping its research terms within the framework of regional *technological poles* and other regional actions.[19] The CNRS has also created assistants in the regions responsible for industrial relations and intensified actions to encourage research workers to accept secondments to industry.

Other important regional technological initiatives in France are:

Agences Régionales d'Information Scientifique et Technique: There are nineteen ARIST, whose funds derive from regional Chambers of Commerce, the state and from their own activities. Their main role is the provision of ST&T information to industry, especially to SMFs.

Centres Régionaux d'Innovations et de Transfert de Technologies: In 1986 there were forty CRITT in place. Their main objectives are to encourage exchanges between public research bodies and industry and to help SMFs to master new technologies and utilize innovative equipment. [20]

Technopoles: Technopoles are grandiose versions of science parks which were established to build upon and enhance regional innovation potentials along established regional technological specialisms. While originally focusing on stimulating technology transfer, more recently they have emphasized the formation of new enterprises. In 1987, there were about fourteen technopoles established with a further three in the planning/construction phases. Most of the infrastructure financing of technopoles has derived from public sector sources. In early 1986 there were 400 establishments on the most advanced technopoles employing between them 10,000 people. [21]

Finally, in 1983 the Délégation de l'Aménagement du Territoire et à l'Action Régionale was established under the direct authority of the Prime Minister. DATAR prepares the agenda for the Inter-Ministerial Committee on Regional Development, which makes the major decisions on regional policy. Since the mid-1970s, funds increasingly have been used for decentralization and are channelled under the Contrats du Plan mechanism. In 1985 expenditure on R&D by regions was FF408 million, about 2.7 per cent of total regional budgets. In 1985 56 per cent of regional R&D budgets was allocated to operations under contract to the state. [22]

In West Germany, the existence of a Federal structure means that the various Lande governments have traditionally played an important role in regional economic development. Increasingly the Lande governments have focused on measures designed to stimulate technology transfer, mainly to SMFs, and to enhance regional technological potentials.

Perhaps the major single technology transfer agency in West Germany is the Fraunhofer Society, which has thirty institutions located in the various regions, whose major function is to perform contract research for industry and government. Contract research income is matched deutschmark for deutschmark with a government subsidy to cover infrastructural maintenance and development. In addition to the general subsidy, aid is available for small firms from the Federal government, amounting to 40 per cent of the costs of projects they commission; it is to help SMFs break through what is considered to be an *entry barrier* to the services of a Fraunhofer institute.

In the mid-1970s the BMFT – Federal Ministry of Research and Technology – and the BMBW – Federal Ministry for Education and Science – initiated several programmes to install technology transfer units at various levels within technical schools and universities:

General Information Transfer Unit: These have a staff of one to four and were installed alongside the administrative staff of various universities and colleges. Examples are the units at Aachen, Berlin, Brekefield, Bechum, Erlongen,

Nüremberg, Fiensberg, Hamburg-Harburg, Karbruke, Kassel, München, Tübirgen and Wiesbaden.

Technology Transfer Officers or Contact Representative: These were installed at colleges without a technology transfer centre. Examples include Braunschwerig, Hamburg, Kaiserlautern and Koblenz.

A number of *regional technology transfer institutions* have also been established. Examples include those set up by the Federal States of Baden Worthenberg and North Rhine-Westphalia. With the aid of financial support from their regional Ministries of Commerce, they are able to subsidize the first two or three consultancies by a small firm to scientists and engineers based within technical colleges.

Other initiatives with regional technology development potential, established specifically to transfer technology to SMFs, are:

technology transfer offices attached to large Federal research establishments.
technology transfer centres attached to applied research institutes; and
innovation consultancy offices, associated with the German Rationalization Board, Chambers of Industry and Commerce and freelance consultants.[23]

Finally, there has been considerable development in Germany towards the establishment of innovation centres/technology parks. These have been initiated by regional and local authorities in an attempt to re-create the models of success that were perceived to exist in places such as Silicon Valley in the USA. In excess of $100 million is said to have been invested in innovation centres between 1981 and 1985, during which period nineteen were established, fourteen were close to being established and forty more were said to be in the pipeline. Those established used over 300 high-tech companies which had a combined employment of 3,000. About 80 per cent or over of funding has been by regional and local governments.[24]

Of the various Federal schemes that exist to nurture the country's base of technology-based firms, the most important to the innovation centres has been the Technology Oriented Enterprise (TOU) programme. This began as a pilot scheme in 1983 and was later expanded to over DM300 million. The TOU programme is aimed at technology-based new businesses throughout Germany, offering grants, loans and loan guarantees. Under the scheme, emerging businesses are seen to pass through three distinct development phases: the *conception* phrase,. for which up to DM454,000 is available to cover up to 90 per cent of the costs of market analysis, etc.; the *development* phase, for which up to DM900,000 is available to cover 75 per cent of R&D and testing costs, etc.; and the *production* phase, for which guarantees on 80 per cent of loans up to DM2 million are available. Fifteen innovation centres have been awarded the power to grant such aid and the majority of innovation centre/technology park companies have assessed and are hoping to assess TOU funds.

Given that most of the regional development initiatives described above are fairly young, that few have been subjected to systematic and objective evaluation, and the lack of time series data on technological potential in the various regions concerned, it is difficult to make any balanced judgements regarding their relative success. Essentially, these initiatives are directed towards inducing structural industrial and economic changes in the regions in which they operate, and such structural changes take many years to manifest themselves in measurable data terms. However, given the relatively greater size and coherence of the initiatives underway in France and West Germany, it would be surprising if the effects of regional renewal policies did not manifest themselves in substantially increased regional economic growth rates in these countries sooner than in the UK.

PUBLIC POLICY AND CORPORATE TECHNOLOGY STRATEGIES

As we have seen, there are broad differences in the approaches European governments adopt in their policies towards innovation. Despite the fact that many of the economic and technological pressures facing Europe are common, differing political philosophies in individual countries manifest themselves in dissimilar public policies. This applies particularly to those policies which are designed to intervene in, and amend, the strategies of private companies. However, while few European governments rest easily with such explicit intervention – and some, like the British, consider it anathema – there are examples of public policies designed, implicitly at least, to influence corporate strategies. The impact of two of these policies on corporate strategies, the UK's Alvey Programme and the EC's ESPRIT, will now briefly be described.

The Alvey Programme has already been discussed. While it has been criticized on a number of fronts, for example for being too *technologically led* rather than *market aware*, and not being value for money, i.e. producing immediate tangible returns, one of the official evaluators of the programme does describe some of its beneficial consequences for participating companies' strategies. Guy[25] argues that participation in Alvey has helped convince many firms of the benefits of collaboration in pre-competitive research. It has also helped some companies appreciate the value of collaboration and *strategic alliances* with industrial partners in both the UK and in other countries; both within public and private ventures; with the university sector; and in areas other than pre-competitive research, e.g. development, production, marketing, etc.. Furthermore, Guy argues, for some firms the act of thinking through the relevance of Alvey work within the context of existing firm strategies has helped them translate tacit agreements as to the nature of these strategies into more explicit, articulated policies. Alvey helped firms decide on the relevance of the particular technology areas to its overall business strategy, and has in some cases stimulated a re-think and restructure of the way R&D is organized within the firm. In short, Alvey has had a considerable educative impact on companies' strategic thinking, and while this might not have been the primary intention of the initiative, it might possibly have beneficial consequences for their subsequent competitiveness.

Sharp[26] contends that ESPRIT has played a seminal part in changing attitudes and strategies amongst Europe's top electronics firms and, in this respect, has acted as a catalyst for the rationalization that is currently taking place. She argues that ESPRIT has been vital in a number of respects. First, it has provided an important channel for co-operation:

The need for co-operation should be set in the context of the early 1980s – the fragmented European industry gradually waking up to the realization that it had allowed the US and then the Japanese multinationals to acquire a seemingly dominant technological lead; the increasingly high cost of R&D and initial set up costs in most high-tech sectors, combined with the uncertainties of the shortening product cycle.... There was no alternative but to meet the threat head-on, which in turn meant rapidly acquiring technological capabilities not possessed in-house. Links with US and Japanese firms made sense technologically, but not strategically, since the objective was to decrease rather than to increase technological dependency.'[27]

She ascribes the fact that internal EC firm linkups are increasing relative to EC–US linkups in part to the existence of programmes such as ESPRIT.

Second, ESPRIT has provided a mechanism for creating amongst top decision-takers convergent expectations about the future, and about the sort of measures needed to meet the competitive threat from US and Japanese multinationals. This shared awareness, she argues, did not effectively exist prior to the formulation of ESPRIT. Third, the programme has created an important constituency pressing for the completion of the internal market and the abolition of all remaining internal barriers to trade, such as divergent standards and regulations. Fourth, ESPRIT has for many firms provided an important learning process in collaboration.

The above two examples illustrate the ways that public technology policies can influence and amend corporate strategies. There are numerous reasons why corporate technology strategies are of legitimate concern to public policy-makers. The cardinal reason is that in Europe the technological performance of key industrial sectors often depends on the behaviour, or strategies, of a very few companies. In the UK, for example, Patel and Pavitt, by means of an analysis of patenting in the USA, have recently shown that UK technology depends heavily on ICI in chemicals, GEC in electronics and Rolls-Royce in aerospace.[28] Some European countries are even more reliant on single companies, such as Philips in the Netherlands and Volvo in Sweden. Sharp[29] argues that the future of the European electronics industry depends to a great extent on the behaviour of three companies: Philips and Siemens of West Germany, and Thomson of France.

Awareness of corporate technological activities alerts public policy-makers to deficiencies in breadth, depth and time-scale in national and European efforts. It may also reveal the necessity for rationalizing, or at least reducing duplication in, research activities, and enable better analysis and prioritization of public sector R&D. Despite these reasons for public policy-maker awareness and involvement, few governments, particularly those that espouse the suzerainty of the market, enthusiastically endorse direct intervention in the technological affairs of firms. Such intervention is, however, increasingly on the agenda for pan-European policy, and this will undoubtedly increase friction between national and EC technology policy.

Some of the rationale for increased EC-wide co-ordinated technology policy has been described above by Sharp: namely, increased global competition, high R&D and start-up costs. The EC adopts the position that to compete effectively in global markets European technological capacity needs to be marshalled. As we have seen in the case of ESPRIT, this programme has improved the prospect of a *European* response to Japanese and US competition. The political concern of the EC to generate European technology has been seen on a number of occasions. For example, the R&D Director of Philips testifies to the importance of political influences in the formation of the joint Philips–Siemens *Mega-project* in sub-micron semiconductor technology.[30]

The political problems to be addressed in concerning pan-European technological interests with those of nation-states are enormous. While it is often the case that European high-tech firms are globally oriented – domestic markets are too small to produce sufficient returns to cover R&D costs – in some technologies Europe possesses too many competing firms, and there are arguments for rationalization of effort. For example, Europe possesses ten turbine generator manufacturers, compared with two in the USA; eleven telephone exchange manufacturers, compared with four in the USA; and twelve boilermaking producers, compared with six in the USA.[31]

Some of the problems for the EC to develop effective policy and to achieve this rationalization are revealed in Morgan's[32] study of the telecommunications industry. Telecommunications have been the most nationally based of all the electronics sectors, yet as Morgan argues, it is important for the EC to develop a telecommunications strategy so as to harmonize regulatory regimes and technical standards preventing the duplication of R&D, and the overcoming of chauvinistic procurement policies. The complexity and comparative inefficiency of the EC industry is exemplified by the production of switching equipment. The EC has seven digital switching systems being installed, five of which were developed by *national champions* backed by their governments. They have an average price per line ranging between $225 and $500, compared to $100 in the USA. The EC believes that if the number of producers could be reduced to two, the price per line could drop to around $150.

Morgan describes the numerous problems the EC has to overcome to create a coherent telecommunications policy. It has to attain the compliance of nations with radically different domestic policies; between, for example, the UK with its liberal markets and West Germany with its highly protected markets. It has to referee the inevitably contradictory requirements of producers and users of telecoms equipment. It has to negotiate trade agreements with the USA which allow sufficient scope for the development of comparative competitive advantage in European firms, initially within Europe but with a mind to future export, without excluding US competitors and preventing trade wars. It has to deal with the thorny problem of selectivity (which switching system?). And it has to deal with its own internal organizational contradictions between those policy-makers concerned with developing European technological capability, with those concerned with competition policy and the removal of protectionism.

The 1992 date for the establishment of the EC free market has brought many public technology policy/corporate technology strategy problems into sharper relief. To date the EC has focused upon improving *environmental* technological factors, in patenting, standardization and regulation, and on *pre-competitive* R&D. Just how prepared the EC will be pro-actively to attempt directly to influence corporate technological behaviour is a matter for speculation. For those who adhere to the integrated-Europe concept, such as the EC President M. Delors, the 1992 *ideal* may provide a greater legitimacy to attempts to produce pan-European solutions to the problems described above. To others with the strong Euro-aversion, exemplified by Mrs Thatcher, such intervention would not be politically feasible.

Just how meaningful the establishment of the free market will be for corporate technology strategies is open to debate. It may well focus corporate attention on intra-EC marketing and distribution, production, acquisition and merger activity, and these may encompass a technological component. But the position with regard to corporate and intercorporate R&D, and intercorporate technological collaboration and trade, remains unclear. From a global technology perspective, it is the case that few European firms can compete by themselves directly with the technological leaders in the USA and Far East. The question remains whether European firms will face this challenge by collaborating with other European firms, or with the world leaders elsewhere. It is apparent that in some sectors the EC possesses overcapacity and rationalization is required. The question remains, how is this rationalization to occur when national and EC interests conflict. The answer to both these questions lies to a significant extent with the technology strategies adopted by companies. The extent to which these strategies are informed and influenced by the EC post-1992, will depend on where along the intervention/non-intervention spectrum political consensus or agreement, if it is achieved, will lie.

Nineteen ninety-two apart, the EC is playing an increasingly active role in the development of European technology. In order to direct a European response to global competition in technology it needs to comprehend, and occasionally attempt to influence, the technology strategies of major companies. The major companies, aware of the potential political power of the EC, and the attractions of the single market, are increasingly entering the European political arena. In electronics, for example, the *Big Twelve*: GEC, Plessey and STC-ICL of the UK; Siemens, Nixdorf and AEG of West Germany; Thomson, CGE and Bull of France, Olivetti and Stet of Italy; and Philips of the Netherlands, have formed the so-called Round Table, an effective, Europe-wide lobby group. How effective the EC will be in marshalling the efforts of such companies – given that they frequently compete in similar markets, and given the extent of individual national interest – remains to be seen. However, the EC is being seen to take an active role in areas such as corporate mergers, and the Framework Programme is by any measure a significant attempt to co-ordinate elements of European R&D. While major political hurdles have to be overcome, the EC will be important in the future development of technology policy, and this policy will encompass and affect corporate technology strategies.

SUMMARY

(*i*) Despite historical differences in approach to public technology policy formulation, and differences in the role of the state in directly influencing industrial technological change, during the 1980s there has been some convergence amongst major European nations in both the nature and focus of technology policies.

(*ii*) Since the mid-1970s there has been an increased emphasis on policies to stimulate innovation in SMFs. During the 1980s small firm policy has focused specifically on stimulating the creation and growth of NTBFs. One result of this policy shift has been a rapid growth in both the volume and availability of venture capital in Europe.

(*iii*) During the 1980s most major European nations have introduced major national programmes of pre-competitive research in information technology which involve collaboration between companies and between companies and universities. These national policies have been complemented by similar policies introduced by the EC which mandate collaboration across national boundaries.

(*iv*) Because of increased concern over growing regional economic disparities, considerable attention was focused during the 1980s on technology-oriented policies designed to increase the technological potential of the less-developed regions. These endogenous regional technology policies have mainly involved the creation and enhancement of regional technology transfer infrastructures.

(*v*) While in France and West Germany coherent regional technology policies are well developed, supported through both central and local government finance, in the UK such policies are in the infant stage. This at least partially reflects the *hands-off* approach adopted by the current political administration in the UK. On the other hand, there are three well-established regional development agencies in the UK (Scottish, Welsh, Northern Irish) which increasingly are focusing on technological change as a core feature in their developmental activities.

(*vi*) An important aspect of corporate behaviour – the strategic management of technology – can be, and is, affected by public policies. Even in the UK, with its ardent anti-interventionist ethos, policies have been introduced which have tangible impacts on firms' strategies for technological collaboration.

(*vii*) Improving the scope and scale of technological collaboration in industry has also been an intention of many EC programmes. In the case of electronics, the EC has been both a catalyst and a focus for the activities of large corporations.

(*viii*) While the EC is attempting to marshall European corporate activity to enable a more coherent and targeted response to global competition, a great many political obstacles need to be overcome before this is achieved. European policies designed to rationalize and offer selective support to key technologies and firms are almost inevitably bound to offend some national interests. It will take many years, and a much more profound cohesion to the European ideal of an integrated S&T community to overcome these political conflicts. The extent to which the consequences of the free market, to be established in Europe in 1992, resulting from tangible improvements of symbolism, modify corporate technological activities remain unclear, and will remain so until after it has been established.

Section 5:

Conclusions

9 Implications of free trade for science and technology policy: the issues and the choices

Louis Marc Ducharme and John de la Mothe

Clearly, today's world economic environment is being re-structured. Contrary to popular perception, however, '1992' will not represent the culmination of this re-structuring but is instead only one part of an ongoing process. The *raison d' être* behind this process can be found in the desire of firms and nations to compete economically. It is for this reason alone that we see the rampant rhetoric and resolve concerning free trade, globalization of markets and globalization of technologies. Competitors want to be winners. In order for this wish to be realized in the contemporary context, however, it is no longer sufficient (or possible) to rely on domestic markets, domestic skill sets, or domestic scientific or technological capabilities. No one country or firm can 'do it all'. Investment and risk in R&D is high. Product development and launch is expensive. Today firms and nations more than ever before need to access new markets, new capital, new technologies and new ideas. But increasingly they also need to rely economically on their allies and competitors to share the risk of innovation. It is for these basic reasons that the world's industrialized economies are re-ordering themselves into new competitive blocks. These nations are learning to co-operate in order to compete. Yet this in itself will not spell success for firms, nations or blocks.

Setting the winning combination will depend on a variety of factors. Propensity to innovate technologically is one important factor, as is the existing trading profile. But it will also depend on the openness of the economy, the market and policy mechanisms which provide incentives to create and innovate, the level of technological accumulation, the ability of the economy to adopt and diffuse new technologies, the ability of the science system to respond and contribute to a changing global environment, and the ability of an economy to identify and narrow existing technological and economic gaps within and between sectors. All these factors, which are discussed at some length in this book, interrelate in a highly dynamic process.

However, it is these factors which, together, establish the terms and likely success of 'going global'. Depending on a nation's existing endowments and capabilities, differing opportunities, issues and choices will arise which dictate the range of possible responses. No two nations or blocks will have exactly the same options. However, trends can be discerned.

Clearly, the challenging project of 'Europe 1992' must be contextualized within the economic re-structuring which began more than thirty years ago. However, the renewed push towards a single market stems from a desire – within the face of heightened international competition – to achieve greater efficiencies in capital and labour mobility, as well as to influence the creation of new 'poles' of growth. Ability to use and apply technology rapidly will clearly be an important factor in competitive success.

Perhaps the most impressive example of these pressures is West Germany when coupled with the collapse of a rigid economic system in East Germany and the Eastern Bloc countries. Already the flow of skilled labour from East to West Germany is threatening to make France and UK pale in terms of their combined perceived potential. Moreover, the opening up of the Eastern Bloc countries will rapidly provide the West with new market opportunities to develop. The plea for a 'Marshall Plan' for Eastern Europe has also been well received by both the EC and by West Germany. The implications of these developments are tremendous. For example, a re-unified Germany promises the return of that country to a central and prominent role in the future growth potential of European and global markets.

For Southern Europe, the challenges are even bigger. The only strategy open to them is one of 'catching up'. The institutional, historical and technological inertias are great. They will have to face the steepness of learning curves as well as of economies of scale. They will have to face the entry barriers to technologies which are put in place by large foreign firms and which are features of established sectors. On the other hand, however, they are not encumbered to the same extent as the highly industrialized nations by the problems associated with trying to shift employment and investment away from the mature industries. The ultimate challenge will be to build or keep at least a threshold level of technical expertise and political-institutional capability in order to impede the reallocation of comparative advantage to other regions of Europe.

In the case of Japan, there can be no doubt that it has had a remarkable post-war economic and trade performance. However, Japan too is at a turning point. It must open its internal markets to competition while at the same time establishing new markets for itself in Asia, Latin America and Africa. It must also develop and demonstrate its ability not only to imitate technologically but also to create technology. If it can do so (and there is strong evidence to show that it is beginning to) Japan may well succeed in extending its own considerable achievements into the twenty-first century and, in so doing, lead the development of a new global economic balance of power. It is to the dynamism of Japan and Northern Europe, as well as to the threshold desires of Southern Europe, that the North American trading block will have to respond if it is to regain a decisive leadership position in this global re-structuring.

Although the USA has been admittedly in a period of economic decline and has come under the tacit threat of losing its technological edge, the Canada–USA Free Trade Agreement stands as evidence that the USA is beginning to take market development and the trade in technology (both exports and imports) seriously. Expectation is that the mobility of research personnel between the two countries will also increase as the FTA becomes more fully operational. Other expectations include an increase of collaborative and contract research between firms and universities on both sides of the border. Further evidence of the USA's interest in world restructuring and technology can be found in the recent moves of substantial R&D capabilities from IBM, Dupont, Hewlett Packard and other industrial giants into European bases, as well as in the government's formal plans in signing a free trade agreement with Mexico. All of this suggests that the USA has already begun to make the connection between science, technology and winning in a free trade environment. While all this is true, however, there is concern within Canada that, because of its narrow industrial profile and young scientific system, the new US influence may impede the technological maturation of the domestic economy.

Within this context the choices are simple. A nation can either act quickly to re-structure internal production capabilities, enhance capital flow mechanisms as well as create the means for sustaining technological presence, or it can let the market forces decide what its economic future will be. The issues, on the other hand, are far from simple. Although we do believe that the market has a clear role to play in allocating resources, it is doubtful that it can foresee, directly encourage or accommodate all of the necessary economic, social and technological transformations that will result in a free market. The role of government will continue to be crucial, if not decisive, in achieving the level of co-ordination and collaboration that is needed between firms, universities and government agencies at all levels.

It is clearly impossible to predict with certainty the precise outcomes that free trade will have on firms, industries, regions or countries. Similarly, the degree to which bureaucracies and cultural attitudes can accommodate economic restructuring can only be a subject for speculation. Nevertheless, what this book has argued is that science and technology will continue to increase in economic and geopolitical importance. In so doing, science and technology policies – and the factors which combine to support and define them – must become an important element in the development of any competitive strategy under free trade. To be sure, the determinants of technological change are complex and may not manifest themselves in all situations. But they do form the basis upon which Schumpeterian efficiencies – which feature sustainable development and sustainable policies – can be designed. We view this important observation as not only acting as a guide to policy-makers and politicians who are responsible for industrial and foreign policy. We see it as also determining the factors which will allow nations to transform their economic bases and relationships. As such, within a free trade environment, the question must ultimately be asked, 'free trade and economic transformation for whom?' If free trade is truly to live up to the industrialized nations' vision of a scientifically and technologically robust paradigm for the twenty-first century, then North–South relations must be conceived in terms which break the vicious circle of sustained impoverishment in favour of sustained technological and economic development.

Epilogue

Michael Gibbons

This volume makes an important contribution to the current debate about the relationship between competitiveness and free trade. Recent events in Eastern Europe, the progress towards a single European market in 1992 and the emergence of an American/Canadian Free Trade Agreement are among the developments that are focusing attention upon the problems and opportunities created by dynamic, interconnected, global markets. There are good reasons for this interest because, to the extent that markets are genuinely free, they carry with them an imperative for change – and there are few individuals or institutions who are able to face the prospect of change with equanimity. It is, therefore, never a mistake to be cautious when the rhetoric of change is enjoying the political and economic limelight that it is today for it often betrays a deep-seated determination to pursue 'business as usual'.

While it may be readily admitted that the desire for change is not natural for the human species, change is nonetheless a necessary condition for continued prosperity in an industrial, market economy. It is the possibility that new commercial opportunities will arise spontaneously that characterizes the market process. It is the subsequent adoption and gradual diffusion of new products and processes that inevitably results in structural change in the economy. The prospects of opening up markets through the development of policies for free trade both increases the number of opportunities for institutional and individual entrepreneurs and heightens the tension arising from the perception that existing ways of doing things may be under threat.

The novel dimension in the current geo-political situation – and it is extremely well documented in this volume – is the technological one; the awareness that many, if not most, of the new commercial opportunities presented by the opening up of free trade will have a distinct technological aspect. Opportunities to apply new technology, either to established ways of doing things or (more radically) to the launching of entirely new firms, will arise rapidly. Of course, the application of technology to the productive process is not a new notion – indeed it is at the core of what is meant by the term 'industry'. Nonetheless, there are times – such as now – when processes of technological 'ripeness' seem to open up a vast range of commercial possibilities which lead to the creation of new technological paradigms and to the destruction of old ones.

Creative destruction, as Schumpeter called it, refers to a process of dynamic competition in which technological change and economic development are inextricably linked; it is a process in which technological change is endogenous rather than exogenous to the economic process. The roots of this form of competition are rivalry, and rivalrous behaviour must produce losers as well as winners. (This volume is especially articulate in discussing this aspect.) In this view it is entrepreneurial alertness acting on technological and commercial opportiunities that constantly moves the economy away from that unvarying state of rest that is described in the economic text books as 'perfect competition'. Policies to promote free trade will enhance competition, but to the degree that these policies are successful they will also promote widespread experimentation in both technical and commercial realms.

This process of experimentation takes place in what Hayek called 'an extended order' – a catallaxy – the principal characteristic of which is that it functions despite the fact that no one single person, firm or institution possesses all the relevant information needed to steer it. An extended order is a vast system of exchanges which has no other purpose than to provide a structured context in which individuals can operate. The most familiar extended order is, of course, the market in which businessmen, entrepreneurs and industrialists make decisions on the basis of partial information. But this partial information nonetheless allows them to achieve their objectives and the objectives of countless thousands of others about whose aims and objectives they are completely ignorant. An analogous situation pertains in the production of scientific and technological knowledge. No one can know all physics or chemistry, or biotechnology or computing, that is – in principle – available. As with economic relations, the scientific and technological enterprise grows by experimentation and specialization. It is scientific entrepreneurs who perceive the cognitive opportunities which open up new paths for the enterprise but no one can predict, much less plan, for their emergence. To some extent then, scientific and technological activities take place within an extended order and such an order, whether in economics or science, functions *both* as a discovery procedure and a coordinating device. An extended order can be regarded as a selection mechanism which exhibits spontaneity and allows the emergence of new products and processes in economic life on the one hand, and novel series and science on the other. In both cases, it is the pressure of competition transmitted through the extended order that promotes innovation by guiding individuals towards the relevant information.

The economic producing orders and knowledge producing orders have now inter-penetrated to the point where it is almost acceptable to regard research results as tradeable commodities whose flows can both stimulate and be stimulated by more conventional market signals. The course of this development would be fascinating to chart but it must be in no small part attributable to the sheer growth in the numbers of knowledge producers over the past fifty years. Further, many of these knowledge producers (perhaps most) are now employed in a wide range of industrial and commercial organizations and their numbers are so large and their ethos so pervasive that they are bound to have affected the reorganization of work along lines related to knowledge acquisition and production. Something like this process must underly the multifaceted set of relationships that connect universities, private and public laboratories, consultancies and so forth in what is now a global extended order. One result of this development is the recognition that access to specific types of knowledge can give firms a temporary differential advantage over their competitors. Firms are coming to realize that maintenance of their knowledge base is as important an element in their long-term survival as investment in new plant and machinery.

Both the public science system and the private techno-economic system have the characteristics of extended orders; that is, they function as markets each driven by its own specific type of competitive behaviour in pursuit of its own objectives, creativity and profit respectively. Since competition normally has the effect of producing winners and losers, it is to be expected that winners will not only dominate the marketplace but will also dictate which technologies will, through standards settings and diffusion, be at the vanguard of industrial structural change. However, such is the nature of an extended order that spontaneously produces new ideas, theories, techniques and so on, for most firms there is an everpresent threat to their established position not only from imitators but also, and more importantly, from other heretofore unknown knowledge centres which may discover new, better or more efficient ways to meet a commercial opportunity based upon a new technology. It is thus hardly surprising that firms can argue persuasively for free trade while developing (or allowing to be developed) policies relating to intellectual property, rights publication, and the flow of information which might guarantee their position just a little longer.

There is no getting around the fact that competition in the marketplace will behave in something resembling an experimental manner and will generate a wide variety of theories, technological paradigms, products, process and so forth. Such variety is essential to any healthy economy because, paradoxically, innovation has the effect of reducing variety. Not only that, but the more successful a given innovation, the more drastically is variety reduced as the losers – those backing other technological standards or solutions to market need – are driven into bankruptcy. A policy and way, then, needs to be found to keep the channels of market experimentation open, and thereby essential variety maintained.

Given that the economic and knowledge generating processes constitute a vast extended order, the most effective way forward is to ensure openness. And yet, the instinctive reaction on the part of many industrialists and government policy makers seems to be to take precisely the opposite path. For example, policies aimed at picking technological winners as a way of supporting faltering industry are not uncommon, yet they fly in the face of what we understand regarding the nature of technological knowledge production. Scientific and technological knowledge productions operates in an extended order; no one possesses all the relevant information or knows whether it exists or could exist if sufficient resources were devoted to it. Therefore, trying to pick technological winners often can distort both the knowledge producing systems as well as the wealth generating processes by reducing variety at the very time that efforts should be made to expand it. Thus policies interested in promoting free trade need to encourage technological diversity and awareness of what the 'significant others' are doing. Of course, using competition to promote variety will produce an inevitable number of losers as well as winners, but this should not discourage efforts. Governments and firms need to find ways to cope with failure in a more positive way. After all, what is the meaning of experimental failure. In its own way such failure produces knowledge of a specific kind and so enters into the fabric of the extended order, perhaps to become useful or relevant later in a currently unsuspected way. The challenge is to learn from experimentation and to set the unsuccessful entrepreneur back on the productive road as soon as possible.

Finally, free trade raises concerns about the roles that government can play in stimulating competition by encouraging firms and industries to pursue more than one line of technological development. If it is true that markets function as heuristic discovery procedures, then the rate of discovery will be enhanced by encouraging firms to pursue distinct paths towards a solution of specific technological problems. For example, by providing resources to the motor industry, governments could encourage different firms to follow fundamentally different technological approaches to, let us say, the problem of lowering emission levels of pollutants. The economic reward would of course go to the firm able to discover and implement the best solution, but the rest of industry would benefit as well through the diffusion of this research-driven solution. Best practice would thereby be enhanced. Much could be learned by examining more closely the ways in which different firms organize their invisible or intangible assets – that is, their knowledge producing resources – as they are marshalled in pursuit of long-term technological goals. The way forward is not to pick 'winners' but to establish policy and strategic processes which allow *a stream* of winners to emerge. This book has carefully, and articulately, examined the ways in which this might be done.

Notes

Chapter 1

1. Evidence of this can be seen by the existence of such free trade groups and agreements as the European Free Trade Association, the Australian – New Zealand Closer Economic Relations Trade Agreement, the Canada – USA Free Trade Agreement, the Latin American Free Trade Association, the Central American Common Market, the Association of South-East Asian nations, the Ireland – United Kingdom Free Trade Agreement and the USA – Israel Agreement.

Chapter 2

1. Johnson (1975).
2. In the OECD Report's words: 'Both the need for adjustment and the possibilities of achieving it are strongly influenced by the underlying pace and directions of technological change, by it rates of diffusion within different national economies, and by the ease with which the technology is transferred from one country to another ... The countries of the OECD have become partners in a world system of dynamic interdependence based upon continued innovation and the unimpeded flow of technology within and across frontiers. In such a system, successful adjustment will depend on the ability of governments to mobilize the inventive, entrepreneurial talents of their people by creating an appropriate climate for technological innovation.' OECD (1979, p. 44).
3. Economic Report of the President (1989) Transmitted to the Congress, Washington, January.
4. According to the 1980 Report of the President on US Competitiveness: 'Many indicators of US trade competiveness such as export market shares suggest that there has been an erosion of US competitiveness in world markets. The increased international competition facing US producers is mainly the result of changing world resource supplies and technological capabilities. Because of higher rates of growth in investment and expanded research activity in other countries, the United States has experienced a relative decline in its trade performance over the past two decades even

though the level of US exports has increased substantially in recent years.' US Department of Labour, Report of the President on US Competitiveness (1980, p. 1–1, 1–2).

5. Vernon, R. (ed.) (1970) *The Technology Factor in International Trade*, BNER/Columbia University Press, New York, p. 2.

6. Krugman, P. (ed.) (1986) *Strategic Trade Policy and the New International Economic*, The MIT Press, Cambridge, Mass.

7. Dixit, A.K. (1986) 'Trade Policy: an Agenda for Research' in Krugman, P. (ed.) (1986) *Strategic Trade Policy and the New International Economic*, The MIT Press, Cambridge, Mass.

8. Pavitt, K. (1984) 'Sectoral Pattern of Technical Change: Towards a Taxonomy and a Theory', *Research Policy*, 13(6), pp. 343–73.

9. Nelson, R. (1981) 'Research on Productivity Growth and Productivity Difference: Dead Ends and New Departures', *Journal of Economic Literature*, 19(3), September, pp. 1029–64.

10. Steedman (1979) and (1980).

11. Dosi, G., Pavitt, K. and Soete, L. (1990) *The Economics of Technical Change and International Trade*, Wheatsheaf, Brighton (forthcoming); Cimoli and Soete (1988).

12. Dosi, G. and Soete, L. (1983) 'Technology Gaps and Cost-Based Adjustments: Some Explorations on the Determinants of International Competitiveness', *Metroeconomica*, 35, pp. 197–222.

13. Nelson, R. and Winter, S. (1982) *An Evolutionary Theory of Economic Change*, The Belknap Press of Harvard University, Cambridge, Mass., p. 356.

14. Similar assumptions were implicit in the original treatment of international trade by Ricardo: 'No extension of foreign trade will immediately increase the amount of value in a country, although it will very powerfully contribute to increasing the mass of commodities, and therefore the sum of enjoyments. As the value of all foreign goods is measured by the quantity of the produce of our land and labour, which is given in exchange for them, we should have no greater value, if, by the discovery of new markets, we obtained double the quantity of foreign goods in exchange for a given quantity of ours.' Ricardo (1951, p. 128). Since production techniques are given, the 'amount of value in a country' is precisely equivalent to its rates of macroeconomic activity as measured by the degree of utilization of its labour force.

15. Soete, L. (1987) 'The New Emerging Information Technology Sector' in Freeman, C. and Soete, L. (1987) *Technology Change and Full Employment*, Blackwell, Oxford.

Chapter 3

1. See for example, Cohen, S. and Zysman, J. (1987) *Manufacturing Matters: the Myth of the Post-Industrial Economy*, Basic books, New York; Cohen, S., Teece, D., Tyson, L. and Zysman, J. (1984) 'Competiveness', Vol. 3 President's Commission on Industrial Competitiveness, BRIE working paper 8, Berkeley Roundtable on the International Economy, University of California, Berkeley, November; Krugman, P. and Hatsopoulos, G. (1987) 'The Problem of U.S. Competitiveness in Manufacturing', *New England Economic Review*, January–February; Scott, B.R. and Lodge, G. (eds) (1985), *U.S. Competitiveness in the World Economy*, Harvard Business School Press, Boston.

2. Kremp, E. and Mistral, J. (1985) 'Commerce Extérieur Américain: d'où vient, où va le déficit?' Centre d'Études Prospectives et d'Informations Internationales, Vol. 22, Paris.

3. Cohen, S. and Zysman, J. (1987) *Manufacturing Matters: the Myth of the Post-Industrial Economy*, Basic Books, New York.

4. For this perspective on Japanese policy, see Pempel, T.J. 'Japanese Foreign Economic Policy: the Domestic Bases for International Behavior' in Peter Katzenstein (ed.), (1978), *Between Power and Plenty: Foreign Economic Policies of Advanced Industrial States*, Unviersity of Wisconsin Press, Madison.

5. For a detailed discussion of the policy patterns summarized here, see Johnson, C. *MITI and the Japanese Economic Miracle*, Stanford: Stanford University Press, and Yamamura, K. (1982) *Policy and Trade Issues of the Japanese Economy*, University of Washington Press, Seattle.

6. For a discussion of standard IMF policy prescriptions, see Williamson, J. (1982) *The Lending Policies of the International Monetary Fund*, Washington: Institute for International Economics, August; for a discussion of standard World Bank policy prescriptions, see The World Bank, *World Development Reports* for 1983, 1984 and 1985 published for the World Bank by Oxford University Press.

7. For a complete description of the standard models of comparative advantage see, for example, Williamson, J. (1983) *The Open Economy and the World Economy*, Basic Books, New York.

8. See, for example, Brander, J. and Spencer, B. (1983) 'International R&D Rivalry and Industrial Strategy', *Review of Economic Studies*, 50, pp. 707–22.

9. This threefold distinction was suggeested by Krugman, P. in 'Strategic Sectors and International Competition' in Stern, R.M. (ed.) (1987) *U.S. Trade Policies in a Changing World Economy*, MIT Press, Cambridge, Mass.

10. There is a fascinating and compelling application of this argument in a study of the computer industry in Flamm, K. (1987) *Targeting the Computer: Government Support and International Competition*, Brookings Institution, Washington.

11. For an overview of these debates, see Brander, J. 'Shaping Comparative Advantage: Trade Policy, Industrial Policy and Economic Performance' in Lipsey, R.G. and Dobson, W. (eds) (1987), *Shaping Comparative Advantage*, Prentice-Hall, Toronto.

12. For evidence on the empirical difficulties involved, see the various empirical applications of the new trade theory presented in Feenstra, R. (ed.) (1988) *Empirical Research in International Trade*, MIT Press, Cambridge, Mass.

13. Krugman, 'Is Free Trade Passé', *op. cit.*

14. Fukukawa, S., Director General of the International Trade Administration Bureau of MITI, quoted in Freeman, C. (1987) *Technology Policy and Economic Performance: Lessons From Japan*, Pinter Publishers, London.

15. This illustration is adapted from Arthur, W.B. (1987) 'Self-Reinforcing Mechanisms in Economics', Working Paper No. 11, Stanford University, Center for Economic Policy Research, Stanford.

16. Freeman, *op. cit*, p. 35.

17. Stiglitz, J.E. (1987) 'Technological Change, Sunk Costs, and Competition', paper prepared for a conference at the Brookings Institution, December.

18. Schumpeter, J. (1942) *Capitalism, Socialism and Democracy*, Harper, New York.

19. As an illustration, see Dennison, E. (1967) *Why Growth Rates Differ: Postwar Experience in Nine Western Countries*, Brookings Institution, Washington.

20. See, for example, Dosi *et al.* (eds), *Technical Change and Economic Theory*, London: Pinter Publishers; and Dosi, G (1974) *Technical Change and Industrial Transformation*, Macmillan, London and St. Martin's Press, New York.

21. Rosenberg, N. (1982) *Inside the Black Box: Technology and Economics*, Cambridge University Press, New York, pp. 74–6.

22. This term and notion has been used widely in our work. See, for example, Cohen, S. And Zysman, J. (1987) *Manufacturing Matters: the Myth of the Post-Industrial Economy*, Basic Books, New York; and Tyson, L. 'Competitiveness: an Analysis of the Problem and a Perspective on Future Policy', in Starr, M.K. (ed.), (1988), *Global*

Competitiveness: Getting the U.S. Back on Track, W.W. Norton, New York.

23. This type of virtuous interdependence is discussed in greater detail in Krugman, 'Strategic Sectors and International Competition', *op. cit.*

24. Excerpted from Cohen and Zysman (1987) *op. cit.*, pp. 94–7.

25. Abernathy, W.J. (1978) *The Productivity Dilemma: Roadblock to Innovation in the Automobile Industry*, Johns Hopkins University Press, Baltimore.

26. Sabel, C.F. (1982) *Work and Politics: the Division of Labor in Industry*, Cambridge University Press, Cambridge, p. 32. Sabel's work implies but does not directly develop this position.

27. Richard Nelson points out that 'It is important to recognize the essential uncertainties which surround the question – where should R&D resources be allocated – in an industry where technology is advancing rapidly. There generally are a wide number of ways in which the existing technology can be improved, and at least several different paths toward achieving any of these improvements. Ex ante it is uncertain which of the objectives is most worthwhile pursuing, and which of the approaches will prove most successful. Before the fact, aviation experts disagreed on the relative promise of the turboprop and turbojet; those that believed in the long run promise of commercial aircraft designed around turbojet engines were of different minds about where to go forward with a commercial vehicle. Whether and when computers should be transistorized was a topic on which computer designers disagreed; later the extent and timing of adoption of integrated circuit technology in computers was a subject which divided the industry ... The uncertainty that characterizes technological advance in high technology industries warns against premature unhedged commitments to particular expensive projects, at least when it is possible to keep options open. The divergences of opinion suggest that a degree of pluralism of competition among those who place their bets on different ideas, is an important, if wastefeul, aspect of technological advance.' See Nelson, R. (1984) *High-Technology Policies: a Five-Nation Comparison*, American Enterprise Institute for Public Policy Research, Washington.

28. Sapolsky, H. (1982) *The Polaris System Development: Bureaucratic and Programmatic Success in Government*, Harvard University Press, Cambridge, Mass.

29. Sabel, C. (1982) suggests in his imaginative book, that technological development is a product of choice. He argues that case when talking about this transition: 'by the end of the 1980s it is likely that comparable stories, different in substance but with equally uncertain ends, will be told for each of the advanced industrial countries. The reindustrialization debate in the United States, the wave of new-liberalism in Great Britain and nationalization in France, and the discussion of democratization and social ownership of large firms in Sweden are surely just the first signs of an epochal redefinition of markets, technologies, and industrial hierarchies. The outcomes will depend on the daring of the imaginations of trade unions, industrialists, and politicians, and on the ideas of different social classes about how they want to work and live. But as soon as a new system, however shaky, is in place, the scientific thinkers on the Right will tell you everything everywhere, down to the last detail, was determined by the pursuit of efficiency. Scientific thinkers on the Left will say that each group's inevitable pursuit of its interest, determined by its place in the division of labor, is the real explanation. Both will agree that ideas of dignity and honor, the political programs they inform, and the conflicts to which they give rise were only foam on the wave of history. If you have been persuaded by the book you have just read, you will not believe them.' See Sabel (1982) p. 2.

30. For a broad discussion of how a firm's organizational structure and strategies affect its innovativeness and competitiveness, see Nelson, R. and Winter, S. *An Evolutionary Theory of Economic Change*, Belknap, Cambridge, Mass.

31. See, for example, Zysman, J. *Governments, Markets and Growth*, Cornell University Press, Ithaca, NY.

32. Zysman, J. (1982) and OECD (1986) *Innovation Policy in France: a report for the OECD*, OECD, Paris.

33. Freeman, C. (1987) *Technology Policy and Economic Performance: Lessons From Japan*, p. 31.

34. Freeman (1987) p. 63.

35. See also Freeman, C. and Soete, L. (1982) *Unemployment and Technical Innovation: a Study of Long Waves in Economic Development*, Pinter Publishers, London.

36. Freeman (1987) p. 64. See also Dosi, G. (1982) 'Technological Paradigms and Technological Trajectories', *Research Policy*, 11, pp. 147–62; and Nelson, R. and Winter, S. (1977) 'The Search for a Useful Theory of Innovation', *Research Policy*, 6, pp. 36–66.

37. Note that when even the film industry begins to be discussed in these new terms, more than a set of technological changes are occurring. Certainly an academic fad is in motion. However, that intellectual fad also seems to be at work in industry as well.

38. The reality of such a shift is reflected in literature as diverse as left-wing social commentary and the *Harvard Business Review*.

Chapter 4

1. Arrow, J.K. *Economic Welfare and the Allocation of Resources for Invention,* in Nelson, R. (ed.) (1962), *The Rate and Direction of Innovative Activity*, NBER, Princeton University Press, Princeton.

2. Kodama, F. (1989) *How Research Investment Decisions Are Made in Japanese Industry*, in CIBA Foundation, *The Evaluation of Scientific Research*, London, Wiley.

3. Itami, H. (1987) *Mobilizing Invisible Assets*, Harvard University Press, Cambridge, Mass.

4. Polanyi, M. (1965) *The Tacit Dimension*, Routledge and Kegan Paul, London.

5. Von Hippel, E. (1987) 'Co-operation Between Rivals: Information Knowhow Trading, *Research Policy*, 16, pp. 219–302.

6. Metcalfe, J.S. (1986) *After Alvey: the Economics of Collaborative Research and Industrial Competition in Advanced IT*, PREST; Georghiou, L. (1989) *Evaluating the Impact of International Collaboration on National R&D*, Paper presented to United Nations Economic Commission for Europe, *Seminar on Evaluation in the Management of R&D*, Madrid, 3–7 April 1989.

7. Van Rossum, W. (1986) *The Effects of Research Council Policies Upon Research Priorities: the Political Economy of Research Councils*, Paper, Annual Meeting, Society for Society Studies of Science, Pittsburgh.

8. Malmborg, C. *et al.* (1988) *Evaluation of the Biomolecular Engineering Programme – BEP (1982–1986) and the Biotechnology Action Programme – BAP (1985–1990) Commission of the European Communities, 1988.*

9. Merton, R.K. (1942) 'Science and Technology in a Democratic Order', *Journal of Legal and Political Sociology*, 1.

10. MacDonald, S.

Chapter 5

1. Soete, L. (1981) 'A General Test of Technological Gap Trade Theory', *Review of World Economics*, 117, pp. 638–66.

2. Bell, M. and Scott-Kemmis, D. (1985) 'A Study of Technology Transfer and the Accumulation of Technological Capacity in Manufacturing Industry in Thailand',

World Bank, Washington; and Katz, J. (1985) 'Domestic Technological Innovations and Dynamic Comparative Advantages' in Rosenberg, N. and Frischtak, J. (eds), *International Technology Transfer*, Praeger, New York.

3. Gibbons, M. and Johnston, R. (1974) 'The Roles of Science in Technological Innovation', *Research Policy*, 3, pp. 220–43.

4. Pavitt, K. (1984) 'Sectoral Patterns of Technical Change: Towards a Taxonomy and a Theory', *Research Policy*, 13, pp. 343–73.

5. Atkinson, A. and Stiglitz, J. (1969) 'A New View of Technological Change', *Economic Journal*, 78, pp. 573–8.

6. On the stability over time in the sectoral patterns of technological activities of individual countries, see reference 14 below; on individual firms, see reference 12.

7. This is reflected in perceptions that patent protection is irreplaceable as a barrier to imitation only in firms in pharmaceuticals and other fine chemicals, where products are technologically easy to copy and manufacture, once developed and tested. See Levin, R., Klevorick, A., Nelson, R. and Winter, S. (1987) 'Appropriating the Returns from Industrial Research and Development', *Brookings Paper on Economic Activity*, 3; Bertin, G. and Wyatt, S. (1988) *Multinationals and Industrial Property*, Wheatsheaf, Brighton.

8. Pavitt, K., Robson, M. and Townsend, J. (1988) 'Technological Accumulation, Diversification and Organization in UK Companies, 1945–83', *Management Science*, 35(1), pp. 81–99.

9. Patel, P. and Pavitt, K. (1987) 'Is Western Europe Losing the Technological Race?', *Research Policy*, 16, pp. 59–85.

10. *Ibid.*

11. Patel, P. and Soete, L. (1989) 'International Comparisons of Activity in Fast-Growing Patent Fields', Science Policy Research Unit, University of Sussex.

12. Narin, F. and Olivastro, D. (1987) *Identifying Areas of Strength and Excellence in UK Technology*, Second Interim Report, CHI Research, New Jersey.

13. *Ibid.*

14. Levin, R., Cohen, W. and Mowery, D. (1985) 'R&D, Appropriability, Opportunity and Market Structure: New Evidence on the Schumpeterian Hypothesis', *American Economic Review*, 75(2).

15. Patel, P. and Pavitt, K. (1989) 'Technological Accumulation in France: What The Patent Statistics Show', *Revue de L'Économie Industrielle*.

16. Pavitt, K. (1988) 'International Patterns of Technological Accumulation' in Hood, N. and Vahlne, J-E (eds), *Strategies in Global Competition*, Croom Helm, London.

17. Schmookler, J. (1966) *Invention and Economic Growth*, Harvard University Press, Cambridge, Mass; Rosenberg, N. (1982) Inside the Black Box, Cambridge University Press, Cambridge.

18. Patel, P. and Pavitt, K. (1989) 'Large Firms in Western Europe's Technological Competitiveness', in Matsson, L. and Stymme, B. (eds), *Corporate and Industry Strategies for Europe*, Routledge, London.

19. See reference 9.

20. Pavitt, K. and Patel, P. (1988) 'The International Distribution and Determinants of Technological Activities', *Oxford Review of Economic Policy*, 4, pp. 35–55.

21. Stiglitz, J. (1987) 'Learning to Learn, Localized Learning and Technological Progress' in Dasgupta, P. and Stoneman, P. (eds), *Economic Policy and Technological Performance*, Cambridge University Press, Cambridge, 1987, pp. 125–53.

22. Abernathy, C. and Hayes, J. (1980) 'Managing our Way to Economic Decline', *Harvard Business Review*, July–August.

23. See reference 8.

24. Prais, S. (1981) *Productivity and Industrial Structure* Cambridge University Press,

Cambridge; Mansfield, E. (1987) 'The Diffusion of Industrial Robots in Japan and the USA' (mimeo), University of Pennsylvania; Haywood, B. (1988) 'The Use of Flexible Manufacturing in Sweden: Some Questions Posed for the United Kingdom?' (mimeo), Brighton Polytechnic.

25. Swords-Isherwood, N. (1980) 'British Management Compared' in Pavitt, K. (ed.) *Technical Innovation and British Economic Performance*, Macmillan, pp. 88–9; Pratten, C. (1976) *A Comparison of the Performance of Swedish and U.K. Companies*, Cambridge University Press, Cambridge.

26. Sorge, A. and Warner, M. (1980) 'Manpower Training, Manufacturing Organization and Workplace Relations in Great Britain and West Germany', *British Journal of Industrial Relations*, 18; Prais, S. (1981) 'Vocational Qualifications of the Labour Force in Britain and Germany', *National Institute Economic Review*, November; Prais, S. and Wagner, K. (1983) 'Some Practical Aspects of Human Capital Investment: Training Standards in Five Occupations in Britain and Germany', *National Institute Economic Review*, August.

27. See reference 18.

28. Sharp, M. (1989) 'European Technology: Does 1992 Matter?', Papers in Science, Technology and Public Policy, No. 20, SPRU/Imperial College.

Chapter 6

1. Outside the textbooks, some consideration is given to these issues. See for instance, Jorde, T.M. and Teeche, D.J. (1980) 'Innovation and Co-operation: Implication of Commercialization for Anti-trust', *Journal of Economic Perspectives*, (forthcoming); Schmalensee (1988) 'Industrial Economics: an Overview', *The Economic Journal*, 98, September.

2. Stiglitz, J.E. (1987) 'Technical Change, Sunk Costs and Competition', *Brookings Papers on Economic Activity*, 3.

3. Rosenberg, N. (1982) *Inside the Black Box: Technology and Economics*. Cambridge University Press, Cambridge, Mass.

4. For instance, when a new product appears, it is unlikely that the old product will even reappear in the market, regardless of the relative factor price swings that might occur.

5. Teece, D.J. (1982) 'Inter-organizational Requirements of the Innovation Process', *Journal of Managerial and Decision Economics*, xx, pp. 35–42.

6. I define process innovation here as innovation with respect to the production of a particular product. Such innovation generally lowers costs or improves quality.

7. According to William Norris, US corporations were not willing to give collaborative research a try until 'these companies had the hell scared out of them by the Japanese'. Davis, D.B. (1985) 'R&D Consortia: Pooling Industries' Resources', *High Technology*, 42, October.

8. This section and the next are based on Pisano, G.G. and Teece, D.J. (1989) 'Collaborative Arrangements and Global Technology Strategy' in Rosenbloom, R. and Burgelman, R. (eds) (1989) *Technology, Competition and Organization Theory*, JAI Press, New York.

9. Foster, R.N. (1986) *Innovation: the Attacker's Advantage*, Summit, New York.

10. Teece, D.J. (1990) 'Market Entry Strategies for Innovators', *Strategic Management Journal* (forthcoming).

11. Teece, D.J. (1989a) 'Inter-organizational Requirements of the Innovation Process', *op cit.*

12. Winter, S.G. (1984) 'Schumptererian Competition in Alternative Technological Regimes', *Journal of Economic Behavior and Organization*, 5(3–5), September-December, pp. 287–320.

13. Nelson, R.R. and Winter, S.G. (1982) *An Evolutionary Theory of Economic Change*, The Belknap Press of Harvard University Press, Cambridge, Mass.

14. Malerba, F. (1985) *The Semiconductor Business: the Economics of Rapid Growth and Decline*, University of Wisconsin Press, Madison.

15. This poses the issue in static terms. It may well happen that external sourcing strategies adopted in the past deny the firm the ability to develop, at competitive cost, technologies relevant to today's market necessities.

16. Levin, R. *et al.* (1987) 'Appropriating the Returns from industrial R&D', *Brookings Papers on Economic Activity*.

17. According to Von Hippel, E. (1982) ('Appropriability of Innovation Benefit as a Predictor of the Source of Innovation', *Research Policy* 11(2), April, pp. 95–115), the dominance of equipment users as innovators can be explained by their relative appropriability advantage.

18. Williamson, O.E. (1975) *Markets and Hierarchies*, Free Press, New York; Williamson, O.E. (1985) *The Economic Institutions of Capitalism*, Free Press, New York.

19. Arrow, K. (1962) 'Economic Welfare and the Allocation of Resources for Inventions' in Nelson, R.R. (ed.), *The Rate and Direction of Inventive Activity*, Princeton University Press, Princeton, NJ.

20. Teece, D.J. (1981) 'The Market for Know-how and the Efficient International Transfer of Technology', *The Annals of the Academy of Political and Social Science*, November, pp. 81–96.

21. Teece, D.J. (1977) 'Technology Transfer by Multinational Firms: the Resource Cost of Transferring Technological Know-how', *The Economic Journal*, 87, June, pp. 242–61.

22. This section is based in part on Teece, D.J. (1986) 'Profiting from Technological Innovation', *Research Policy*, 15, pp. 286–305; Teece, D.J. (ed.) (1987) *The Competitive Challenge: Strategies for Industrial Innovation and Renewal*, Ballinger Press, Cambridge, Mass.

23. Comment attributed to Peta Olson III (1985) 'The Strategy Behind IBM's Strategic Alliances', *Electronic Business*, 1 October, p. 128, IBM's Director of Business Development.

24. For example, McKenna, R. (1985) 'Market Positioning in High Technology', *California Management Review*, 27(3), Spring.

25. Williamson, O.E. (1975) *Markets and Hierarchies*, Free Press, New York; Teece, D.J. (1977) 'Technology Transfer by Multinational Firms: the Resource Cost of Transferring Technological Know-how', *The Economic Journal*, 87, June, pp. 242–61.

26. Williamson, O.E. (1985) *The Economic Institution of Capitalism*, Free Press, New York, 1985.

Chapter 7

1. An earlier version of this paper was published in John de la Mothe (ed.), 'Science and Technology Policy Under Free Trade', Special issue of *Technology in Society*, Pergamon Press, New York, May 1989. The views expressed herein are those of the author and not of the Manufacturers forum.

2. It is arguable whether any private property can exist in the absence of social convention and enforcement, and one can view intellectual property as simply the most recent social invention to establish the notion of private ownership to meet larger social needs; labour, land and capital being earlier examples.

3. Organization for Economic Co-operation and Development, *Science and Technology Policy Outlook – 1988*, Paris, 1988.

4. It is important in this and subsequent discussions to be clear about the goals of

technology strategy. These remarks focus on its effectiveness in enhancing the position of a nation in comparison with others, not in enhancing the absolute level of development of a nation. In the instant case, basic research, whatever its venue, may enhance the standard of living of every nation, while leaving their relative positions unchanged.

5. The Omnibus Trade and Competitiveness Act of 1988 has several provisions giving preference to US firms in offering technical assistance from the National Institute of Standards and Technology, formerly the National Bureau of Standards. See the latter parts of this paper for further discussion of this matter.

6. Many of SEMATECH's member firms have manufacturing plants overseas, or are engaged in joint ventures with foreign firms to manufacture chips or process equipment. It is not clear whether or how SEMATECH intends to limit the transfer of technology overseas via these members. It is also not clear how SEMATECH intends to respond to the recent report that NEC (Nippon Electric Company) may seek to become a member, especially in view of Article I(1)(B) of the new US–Japan bilateral nations and technology agreement signed on 20 June 1988 in Toronto, that both science will follow the principle of, 'Comparable access to major government-sponsored or government-supported programs and facilities for visiting researchers, and comparable access to and exchange of information, in the field of scientific and technological research and development.'

7. Canadian Department of Finance (1988) Fiscal Policy and Economic Analysis Branch, *The Canada–U.S. Free Trade Agreement: an economic assessment*, Ottawa, 66 pages, undated.

8. Arlene Wilson and Carl E. Behrens, co-ordinators (1988) *The Effect of the Canada-U.S. Free Trade Agreement on U.S. Industries*, Congressional Research Service Report for Congress, 88–506E, 69 pages, 22 July, p. 3.

9. McCurdy, Howard D, (1988) 'Free Trade to Hurt Canadian Research,' *Montreal Gazette*, 16 August.

10. Hill, Christopher T. (1987) 'Conference in Review' in Rudé Eric, (ed.), *Proceedings of the 40th Annual Meeting of the national Conference on the Advancement of Research and 24th Annual Meeting of the Canadian Research Management Association*, pp. 13–20.

11. U.S. National Science Foundation, (1988) *Science and Engineering Indicators 1987*.

12. Holbrook, J.A.D., (1988) Ministry of State for Science and Technology, Ottawa, personal communication based on information from Statistics Canada; Science Technology and Capital Stock Division, September.

13. Statistics Canada (1988) Science, Technology and Capital Stock Division, *Industrial Research and Development Statistics 1986*, July.

14. Holbrook, *op. cit.*

15. Paka, J. and Anderson, A, (1988) 'Underinvestment Lies at the Core', *Nature*, 333, 23 June, p. 719.

16. Maibach, W.D. and Smith, E.T. (1988) 'A Perilous Cutback in Research Spending', *Business Week*, 20 June.

17. *Ibid.*

18. 'R&D in 1988', (1989) *Business Week Innovation in America*, pp. 178–232.

19. John de la Mothe, private communications, based on data in *Financial Post*, 'Research and Development, Special Report', October 3, 1988, and 'Industry's 500', Summer 1989.

20. Holbrook, *op. cit.*

21. *Business Week*, *op. cit.*

22. Holbrook, *op. cit.*

23. U.S. National Science Foundation, *op. cit.*

24. Organization for Economic Co-operation and Development, *Main Economic Indicators*, July 1988; and *Monthly Statistics of Foreign Trade*, July 1988.

25. *Caves, R.C., Porter, M.E. and Spence, A.M., (1980) Competition in the Open Economy: a Model Applied to Canada*, Harvard University Press, Cambridge, Mass.
26. *Ibid.*, p. 175.
27. *Ibid.*, p. 381.
28. *Ibid.*
29. *Ibid.*, p. 167.
30. *Ibid.*, p. 174.
31. Canadian Department of External Affairs (1987) *The Canada-U.S. Free Trade Agreement*, Ottawa, Canada, 10 October.
32. *Ibid.*, p. 230.
33. *Ibid.*, p. 292.
34. Congressional Research Service, *op. cit.*
35. Blumenthal, W.B. (1988) 'The World Economy and Technological Change', *Foreign Affairs*, 66(3), pp. 529–50; Reich, R.B. (1987) 'The Rise of Techno-Nationalism', *The Atlantic Monthly*, 259(63–69), May.
36. Kindleberger, Charles P., (1976) 'Don't Look Back – They Might be Gaining On Us', in *Technological Innovation and Economic Development: Has the U.S. Lost the Initiative?*, Proceedings of a Symposium on Technological Innovation, Energy Research and Development Administration, Washington, DC, 19–20 April, CONF-760491.

Chapter 8

1. Rothwell, R. and Zegveld, W. (1982) *Innovation and the Small and Medium-Sized Firm*, Pinter Publishers, London.
2. Rothwell, R. and Zegveld, W. (1981) *Industrial Innovation and Public Policy*, Pinter Publishers, London.
3. Figures are for 1983.
4. *Ibid.*
5. Rothwell, (1985).
6. Little, A.D. (1977) *New Technology-Based Firms in the UK and the FRG*, Anglo-German Foundation, London.
7. Segal, Quince and Wicksteed and ISI (1986) *New Technology-Based Firms*, SQW, Cambridge.
8. Guy, K. and Arnold, E. (1987) *Government IT Policies in Competing Countries*, Report prepared for the Electronics EDC of the National Economic Development Office, Science Policy Research Unit (mimeo), November.
9. *Ibid.*, pp. 31 and 32.
10. *Ibid.*
11. Sharp, M. (1989a) 'European Technology: Does 1992 Matter?', Science Technology and Public Policy Lecture No. 20, Imperial College, London, 21 February 1989.
12. Andre, M. (1988) *Research and Technology Development Policy*, European Community, Luxembourg.
13. NEDO – National Economic Development Office (1989) *Technology Transfer Mechanisms in the UK and Leading Competitor Nations*, NEDO, London (by Rothwell, R., Dodgson, M. and Lowe, S.).
14. Sharp, M. (1985) *Europe and the New Technologies*, Pinter Publishers, London.
15. Sharp, M. (1985) *The New Biotechnology: European Governments in Search of a Strategy*, Sussex European Paper No. 15, SPRU.
16. NEDO, op.cit.
17. *Financial Times*, 9 December 1986.
18. Sunman, H. (1986) *France and Her Technopoles*, CSP Economic Publications, Cardiff.

19. Sweeney, G. (1985) *Study on Information Networks Designed to Support Technological Innovation in the Less-Favoured Regions of the Community*, Institute for Industrial Research and Standards, Dublin.

20. Sunman (1986) *op. cit.*

21. *Ibid.*

22. *Ibid.*

23. Meyer-Krahmer, F. (1985) 'Government Promotion of Linkages Between Research Institutions and Industry in the FRG', International Seminar on Institutional Linkages in Technological Development, San Paulo, 25–28 November.

24. Sunman, H. and Lowe, J. (1986) *West Germany: Innovation Centres and Science Parks*, CSP Economic Publications, Cardiff.

25. Guy, K. (1989) 'Corporate Strategies and Public Policy – the Case of Alvey Programme', in Dodgson, M. (ed), *Technology Strategy and the Firm: Management and Public Policy*, Longman, Harlow.

26. Sharp, M. (1989b), 'Corporate Strategies and Collaboration – the Case of ESPRIT and European Electronics', in Dodgson, M., *op. cit.*

27. *Ibid.*

28. Patel, P. and Pavitt, P. (1987), 'The Elements of British Technological Competitiveness', *National Institute Economic Review*, November.

29. Sharp, M. (1989b), *op. cit.*

30. Kramer, Dr P., Seminar at Chatham House, London, 29 November 1988

31. *Economist*, 9 July 1988.

32. Morgan, K. (1989), '*Telecom Strategies in Europe: the End of Parochialism?*', *Hostile Brothers: Competition and Closure in the European Electronics Industry*, Chapter 8 of Cawson, A., Morgan, K., Holmes, P., Stevens, A. and Webber, D., Clarendon Press, Oxford.

Bibliography

Abernathy, C. and Hayes, J. (1980) 'Managing our Way to Economic Decline' *Harvard Business Review*, July/August.

Arrow, J.K. (1962) 'Economic Welfare and the Allocation of Resources for Inventions' in Nelson, R.R. (ed.), *The Rate and Direction of Inventive Activity*, Princeton University Press, Princeton, New Jersey.

Atkinson, A. and Stiglitz, J. (1969) 'A New View of Technological Change', *Economic Journal*, 78, pp. 573-8.

Bell, M. and Scott-Kemmis, D. (1985) 'A Study of Technology Transfer and the Accumulation of Technological Capacity in Manufacturing Industry in Thailand'. World Bank, Washington.

Cimoli, M. and Soete, L. (1988) 'A Generalised Technology Gap Trade Model'. A paper prepared for the conference on Technological innovations, Institutions and Organisation, Trieste, September.

Davis, D.B. (1985) 'R&D Consortia: Pooling Industries' Resources' *High Technology*, 42, October, pp. 42-52.

Department of Labour (1980) 'Report of the President on US Competitiveness', Department of Labour, Washington.

Dixit, A.E. (1986) 'Trade Policy: An Agenda for Research' in Krugman, P. (ed.) (1986) *Strategic Trade Policy and New International Economic*, The MIT Press, Cambridge (Mass), pp. 283-304.

Dosi, G. and Soete, L. (1983) 'Technology Gaps and Cost-Based Adjustments: Some Explorations on the Determinants of International Competitiveness' *Metroeconomica*, 35, pp. 197-222.

Dosi, G. Pavitt, K. and Soete, L. (1990) *The Economics of Technical Change and International Trade*, Wheatsheaf, Brighton.

Economic Report of the President (1989), Transmitted to the Congress, Washington, January.

Foster, R.N. (1986) *Innovation: the Attacker's Advantage*, Summit, New York.

Georghiou, L. (1989) *Evaluating the Impact of International Collaboration on National R&D*, Paper presented to United Nations Economic Commission for Europe, *Seminar on Evaluation in the Management of R&D*, Madrid, 3-7 April 1989.

Gibbons, M. and Johnston, R. (1974) 'The Roles of Science in Technological Innovation', *Research Policy*, 3, pp. 220-43.

Haywood, B. (1988) 'The Use of Flexible Manufacturing in Sweden: Some Questions Posed for the United Kingdom?' (mimeo), Brighton Polytechnic.

Itami, H. (1987) *Mobilizing Invisible Assets*, Harvard University Press, Cambridge.

Johnson, H. (1975) 'Technological Change and Comparative Advantage: An Advanced Country's Viewpoint', *The Journal of World Trade Law*.

Jorde, T.M. and Teece, D.J. (1990) 'Innovation and Co-operation: Implication of

Commercialization for Anti-trust', *Journal of Economic Perspectives*, forthcoming.

Katz, J. (1985) 'Domestic Technological Innovations and Dynamic Comparative Advantages' in Rosenberg, N. and Frischtak, J. (eds), *International Technology Transfer*, Praeger, New York.

Kodama, F. (1989) *How Research Investment Decisions Are Made in Japanese Industry*, CIBA Foundation in *The Evaluation of Scientific Research*, Wiley, London.

Krugman, P. (ed.) (1986) *Strategic Trade Policy and the New International Economic*, The MIT Press, Cambridge, Mass.

Levin, R., Klevorick, A. Nelson, R. and Winter, S.G. (1987) 'Appropriating the Returns from Industrial R&D', *Brookings Papers on Economic Activity*.

————, Cohen, W. and Mowery, D. (1985) 'R&D, Appropriability, Opportunity and Market Structure: New Evidence on the Schumpeterian Hypothesis', *American Economic Review*, 75 (2).

Malerba, F. (1985) *The Semiconductor Business: the Economics of Rapid Growth and Decline*, University of Wisconsin Press, Madison.

Malmborg, C. *et al*, (1988) 'Evaluation of the Biomolecular Engineering Programme – BEP (1982–1986) and the Biotechnology Action Programme – BAP (1985–1990)', Commission of the European Communities, 1988.

Mansfield, E. (1987) 'The Diffusion of Industrial Robots in Japan and the USA' (mimeo) University of Pennsylvania.

McKenna, R. (1985) 'Market Positioning in High Technology', *California Management Review*, 27 (3), Spring.

Merton, R.K. (1942) 'Science and Technology in a Democratic Order', *Journal of Legal and Political Sociology*, 1.

Metcalfe, J.S. (1986) *After Alvey: the Economics of Collaborative Research and Industrial Competition in Advanced IT*, PREST.

Narin, F. and Olivastro, D. (1987) *Identifying Areas of Strength and Excellence in UK Technology*, Second Interim Report, CHI Research, New Jersey.

Nelson, R.R. (1981) 'Research on Productivity Growth and Productivity Difference: Dead Ends and New Departures', *Journal of Economic Literature*, 19 (3), September, pp. 1029-64.

Nelson, R.R. and Winter, S.G. (1977) 'In Search of a Useful Theory of Innovation', *Research Policy*, 6 (1).

————, (1982) *An Evolutionary Theory of Economic Change*, The Belknap Press of Harvard University, Cambridge, Mass.

Oakey, R., Rothwell, R. and Cooper, S. (1988) *Management of Innovation in High Technology Small Firms*, Pinter, London.

Olson, P. III (1985) 'The Strategy Behind IBM's Strategic Alliances', *Electronic Business*, 1 October, p. 126.

Pavitt, K. (1984) 'Sectoral Patterns of Technical Change: Towards a Taxonomy and a Theory', *Research Policy*, 13, pp. 343-73.

————, Robson, M. and Townsend, J. (1988) 'Technological Accumulation, Diversification and Organization in UK Companies, 1945-83', *Management Science*,35, (1), pp. 81-99.

————, and Patel, P. (1988) 'The International Distribution and Determinants of Technological Activities', *Oxford Review of Economic Policy*, 4, pp. 35-55.

————, (1988) 'International Patterns of Technological Accumulation', in N. Hood and J-E Vahlne, (ed.), *Strategies in Global Competition*, Croom Helm.

Patel, P. and Pavitt, K. (1987) 'Is Western Europe Losing the Technological Race?', *Research Policy*, 16, pp. 59-85.

————, and Pavitt, K. (1989) 'Large Firms in Western Europe's Technological Competitiveness', in Matsson, L. and Stymme, B. (eds), *Corporate and Industry Strategies for Europe*, Routledge, London.

————, and Soete, L. (1989) 'International Comparisons of Activity in Fast-Growing Patent Fields', Science Policy Research Unit, University of Sussex.

————, and Pavitt, K. (1989) 'Technological Accumulation in France: What the Patent Statistics Show', *Revue de L'Économie Industrielle*.

Perez, C. and Soete, L. (1988) 'Catching Up in Technology: Entry Barriers and Windows of Opportunity', in Dosi, G. *et al* (1988) *Technical Change and Economic Theory*, Pinter Publishers, London.

Pisano, G.G. and Teece, D.J. (1989) 'Collaborative Arrangements and Global Technology Strategy' in Rosenbloom, R. and Burgelman, R. (eds), *Technology, Competition and Organization Theory*, JAI Press, New York.

Polanyi, M. (1965) *The Tacit Dimension*, Routledge and Kegan Paul, London.

Prais, S. (1981) *Productivity and Industrial Structure*, Cambridge University Press, Cambridge.

Prais, S. (1981) 'Vocational Qualifications of the Labour Force in Britain and Germany', *National Institute Economic Review*, November.

Prais, S. and Wagner, K. (1983) 'Some Practical Aspects of Human Capital Investment: Training Standards in Five Occupations in Britain and Germany', *National Institute Economic Review*, August.

Pratten, C. (1976) *A Comparison of the Performance of Swedish and U.K. Companies*, Cambridge University Press, Cambridge.

Ricardo, D. (1951) *On the Principles of Political Economy and Taxation*, Sraffa, P. (ed.), Cambridge University Press, Cambridge.

Rosenberg, N. (1982) *Inside the Black Box: Technology and Economics*, Cambridge University Press, Cambridge.

Rothwell, R. and Zegveld, W. (1981) *Industrial Innovation and Public Policy*, Pinter, London.

————, (1982) *Innovation and Small and Medium Sized Firms*, Pinter, london.

————, (1985) *Reindustrialization and Technology*, Pinter, London.

Schmalensee, R. (1988) 'Industrial Economics: an Overview', *The Economic Journal*, 98, September.

Sharp, M. (1989) 'European Technology: Does 1992 Matter?', Papers in Science, Technology and Public Policy, No. 20, SPRU/Imperial College.

Schmookler, J. (1966) *Invention and Economic Growth*, Harvard University Press, Cambridge, Mass.

Smith, A. (1776) *Wealth of Nations*. Penguin, Harmondsworth.

Soete, L. (1981) 'A General Test of Technological Gap Trade Theory', *Review of World Economics*, 117, pp. 638-66.

————, (1987) 'The Newly Emerging Information Technology Sector' in Freeman, C. and Soete, L. (eds.) (1987) *Technical Change and Full Employment*, Basil Blackwell, Oxford.

Sorge, A. and Warner, M. (1980) 'Manpower Training, Manufacturing Organization and Workplace Relations in Great Britain and West Germany', *British Journal of Industrial Relations*, 18.

Steedman, I. (ed.) (1979) *Fundamental Issues in Trade Theory*, Cambridge University Press, Cambridge.

————, (1980) *Trade Amongst Growing Economies*, Cambridge University Press, Cambridge.

Stiglitz, J.E. (1982) 'Technical Change, Sunk Costs and Competition', *Brookings Papers on Economic Activity*, 3.

————, (1987) 'Learning to Learn, Localized Learning and Technological Progress' in Dasgupta, P. and Stoneman, P. (eds), *Economic Policy and Technological Performance*, Cambridge University Press, Cambridge, 1987, pp. 125-53.

Swords-Isherwood, N. (1980) 'British Management Compared' in Pavitt, K. (ed.), *Technical*

Innovation and British Economic Performance, Macmillan, pp. 88-9.

Teece, D.J. (1977) 'Technology Transfer by Multinational Firms: the Resource Cost of Transferring Technological Know-how', *The Economic Journal*, 87, June, pp. 242-61.

————, (1981) 'The Market for Know-how and the Efficient International Transfer of Technology', *The Annals of the Academy of Political and Social Science*, November, pp. 81-96.

————, (1986) 'Profiting from Technological Innovation', *Research Policy*, 15, pp. 286-305.

————, (ed.) (1987) *The Competitive Challenge: Strategies for Industrial Innovation and Renewal*, Ballinger, Cambridge, Mass.

————, (1989a) 'Interorganizational Requirements of the Innovation Process' *Journal of Managerial and Decision Economics*, 35 (42), pp. 35-42.

————, (1989b) 'Innovation and the Organization of Industry', Working Paper EAP-34, Center for Research in Management, University of California at Berkeley.

————, (1990) 'Market Entry Strategies for Innovators', *Strategic Management Journal*, forthcoming.

van Rossum, W. (1986) *The Effects of Research Council Policies Upon Research Priorities: the Political Economy of Research Councils*, Paper, Annual Meeting of the Society for Social Studies of Science, Pittsburgh.

Vernon, R. (ed.) (1986) *The Technology Factor in International Trade*, NBER/Columbia University Press.

Von Hippel, E. (1982) 'Appropriability of Innovation Benefit as a Predictor of the Source of Innovation', *Research Policy*, 11 (2), April, pp. 95-115.

————, (1987) 'Co-operation Between Rivals: Information Knowhow Trading, *Research Policy*, 16, pp. 219-302.

Williamson, O.E. (1975) *Markets and Hierarchies*, Free Press, New York.

————, (1985) *The Economic Institutions of Capitalism*, Free Press, New York.

Winter, S.G. (1984) 'Schumpeterian Competition in Alternative Technological Regimes', *Journal of Economic Behavior and Organization*, 5 (3-4), September-December, pp. 287-320.

Author Index

Subject Index